LE   Q95

Memorizing was recommended not only by Cicero (seated, right) for students of Rhetoric (whom he represents, and who is standing behind him), but also by Aristotle (seated, left) for students of Dialectic (standing behind him). Details from *The Wisdom of Thomas Aquinas* by Andrea da Firenze, Chapter House of Santa Maria Novella, Florence (Photo: Mansell-Alinari).

ARISTOTLE
ON MEMORY

Richard Sorabji

DUCKWORTH

First published in 1972 by
Gerald Duckworth & Company Limited
43 Gloucester Crescent, London, N.W.1

ISBN 0 7156 0604 2

Printed in Great Britain
by Ebenezer Baylis and Son Ltd.
The Trinity Press, Worcester, and London

TO KATE

Contents

The place system of memory. This set of places to be fixed in the memory comes from a memory treatise of 1520, *Congestorium Artificiosae Memoriae* by Johannes Romberch. A person must first form images in his mind of these places (the buildings and their interiors) in an alphabetically fixed order. When he wishes to memorize the points in a speech, he will form a second set of mental images symbolizing the points. The image symbolizing the first point must be superimposed on the image of the first place, that symbolizing the second on the image of the second, and so on.

Preface

This book has four components. (i) The translation aims at being more faithful to the original than existing English translations. It is hoped this will benefit philosophers, who need to know as exactly as possible how each argument is expressed. But if it succeeds in preserving something of Aristotle's crisp and compressed style, it will serve another purpose as well.

(ii) The italicized headings that are interspersed with the translation are not faithful to Aristotle's words. They involve a good deal more interpretation. The aim has been, as far as possible, to transfer interpretation from the translation itself to these headings.

Part, but only part, of the essays and notes ((iii) and (iv)) is given over to explaining Aristotle's argument, which is quite often hard to follow.

Philosophers may be surprised to find in Aristotle's treatise a philosophical discussion of memory similar to, but often more detailed than, the kind of discussion to be found in the British empiricist tradition. At the same time, they will notice material of a kind that may be quite unfamiliar, for example the treatment of mnemonic systems. The essays and notes discuss both kinds of subject. They do so without assuming knowledge of Greek.

I am most grateful to the many people who helped me in the work on this book, and especially to Professor J. L. Ackrill. Through his kindness, I had the rewarding experience of reading drafts of the translation and notes to the Oxford Aristotelian group, throughout the year, 1968-9. I also had the benefit, outside these meetings, of further critical comment from Professor Ackrill. I had many helpful discussions with former students at Cornell University. And of these I should like to mention in particular Robert Merrihew Adams, Marilyn McCord Adams, Norton Batkin, Jeanette Desor, Teona Dorrien-Smith, Simmie Freeman and Colin Lyas. I benefited from seeing unpublished papers by Professor Norman Malcolm ('Explanations of Memory'), Professor Steven Tigner ('The Gross Structure and Development of Plato's Theory of *Anamnesis*') and Professor Harry Caplan (Presidential address to the American Philological Association). I am grateful for another kind of help to

ix

The Howard Foundation of Brown University for the Fellowship which supported me during 1968–9, to the National Endowment for the Humanities for a project grant (no. H68–0–95), awarded for the same year, and to Cornell University for two summer research grants. The present book represents a part of the work done with this support.

King's College, London   R.R.K.S.
1971

1. Memory

Aristotle's account of memory is fuller than that to be found in the best-known British empiricists. And it therefore serves, for the student, as a better introduction to the subject of memory. Unlike the *De Sensu*, which precedes it in the traditional order, and which is primarily a contribution to science, the treatise on memory is primarily philosophical. It provides an interesting variation on latterday British empiricist ideas. So in this Chapter (but not in the next Chapter, on mnemonics), we shall approach Aristotle with the interests, and from the point of view, of a modern philosopher.

What is included under the heading of memory?

What sort of memory does Aristotle discuss? He uses two verbs for remembering, *mnêmoneuein* and *memnêsthai*. But as he does not seem to intend any distinction between them, they have not been given different translations. A wide range of things may be remembered, for example facts (that one learnt, contemplated, heard, or saw something, 449^{b}20–2; objects of scientific knowledge, 451^{a}29; that one did something the day before yesterday, 452^{b}30–453^{a}1). Again, one may remember a person (450^{b}30–451^{a}1), a name (452^{b}5), the last member of a list of things such as milk, white, mist, fluid, autumn (452^{a}14–16), what one saw or experienced (451^{a}30), how much time has elapsed (452^{b}30), things in mathematics (452^{a}3), objects of thought (450^{a}12–13), events (452^{b}17–22), the past (449^{b}15; ^{b}28).

Dispositional memory

In talking of remembering, one may be talking of something that goes on at a particular time, or one may be talking of a tendency or an ability which lasts over a period of time, and which belongs to a man whether he is awake or asleep. We can for convenience call the first the act of remembering, and the second the disposition. Aristotle's account of the disposition is that it is a *state* or *affection* (*hexis* or *pathos* 449^{b}25; 451^{a}23–4; 451^{a}27–8), that follows on perceiving, apprehending, experiencing, or learning (449^{b}24–5; 451^{a}21–2). It does not count as memory, until a little interval has

1

elapsed (449^{b}25; 451^{a}29–31). The *affection* (450^{a}26; 30; 450^{b}5; 12; 18) turns out to be a sort of imprint stamped in to a bodily organ. But the mere existence of the affection is not enough. The people described at 452^{a}4–12 and 453^{a}14–23 appear to have retained the appropriate quasi-imprint, but none the less to have temporarily lost memory. In addition to the affection (i.e. the quasi-imprint), there is needed a certain *state*. And the state turns out to be (452^{a}10–11) the ability to excite the quasi-imprint and the corresponding mental image.

Aristotle seems to think of the disposition mistakenly as an ability to perform acts of remembering.[1] This in turn leads him to pay more attention to the act of remembering than to the ability, in accordance with the maxim that in order to analyse an ability, one must first analyse the corresponding activity (*DA* 415^{a}14–20).

Let us now consider what Aristotle says about the act of remembering. It is tempting, if somewhat misleading, to ask what goes on when one remembers.

The mental image

When one remembers, the present content of one's mind, according to Aristotle, is a mental image. The idea that such an image is involved is introduced as something that is 'clear' (450^{a}27). We shall want to know what makes it so clear to Aristotle.

But first we should notice that Aristotle's theory of remembering requires not any kind of image, but an image that is a likeness or copy (*eikôn* 450^{b}27; 451^{a}2; ^{a}11–12) of the thing remembered. An *eikôn* of X, strictly speaking, is both similar to, and derived from, X.[2] The kind of derivation that Aristotle has in the front of his mind is the causal one described in 450^{a}27–^{b}11. The image is causally

---

[1] Mistakenly, for if we say of a child who once burnt himself on the stove, 'he remembers nowadays that the stove is hot', we may simply be implying that because of his unpleasant experience he nowadays tends to avoid touching the stove. This cannot easily be called an ability or tendency to perform acts of remembering. An act of jerking one's hand away from the stove might in certain contexts be called an act of remembering. But if the child merely refrains over a period from touching the stove, because of his unpleasant experience, this cannot very naturally be called an act, or a series of acts, of remembering.

[2] See Cornford's useful comments on pp. 93–4 of *Plato and Parmenides*. In the translation below, *eikôn* is rendered as 'copy', and *phantasma* as 'image' (i.e. mental image). At one point, Aristotle qualifies his statement, by calling the memory image only *a sort of eikôn* (450^{b}27).

derived from a past act of perceiving and from the corresponding object of perception. Whether one is remembering may depend on whether one's image is an *eikôn* (451ª2–5; ª8–12).

This seems to be a correct account of one kind of case.[1] But we must protest against Aristotle that it is not the only kind. Insofar as images are used at all in remembering, they need not necessarily be likenesses of what is remembered. They can be in varying degrees symbolic and unlike. (In some of these cases, it is more appropriate to speak of them as images *for*, rather than as images *of*, what is remembered.) When a memory image of (or for) a man is not a likeness of him, it may for example be a likeness of something which exists in association with him (his moustache), or a likeness of something I think of in association with him (an elephant, if he's Indian), or a likeness of something which I deliberately make to stand for him (an anvil, if his name is Smith). In these cases, the image has a double reference. On the one hand, it is an image (and a likeness) of a moustache, an elephant, or an anvil. On the other hand, it is an image (but not a likeness) of (or for) the man. The images which are devised in mnemonic systems, to stand for the objects that are being memorized, are often very unlike those objects. In the *Rhetorica ad Herennium*, for example (III.20), we are advised to use an image of testicles to represent, punningly, the witnesses (*testes*) in a lawsuit. In view of Aristotle's interest in mnemonics, we might have expected him to deal with this kind of symbolization. But he does not seem to do so.[2]

---

[1] The kind of case which fits Aristotle's account best is one in which one tries to remember what something looked like by conjuring up a mental picture of it. In such a case, whether one succeeds in remembering may depend on whether one's image is like the thing. Thus an instructor may try to remember which student it was who produced a certain performance, by conjuring up an image of the student. The image resembles a tall, blond man without spectacles, and he takes it that the student in question has these features. If it turns out that the student who produced the performance is in fact short, swarthy and bespectacled, the instructor may have to agree that he is not remembering the right man.

[2] When he says that remembering involves an *eikôn*, he means an *eikôn* of the thing remembered, not of some symbol for it. Thus at 450ᵇ13, he speaks of our remembering the thing from which our image is derived, not of our remembering something merely associated with that thing. Again, he does not have in mind symbolic associations at 451ª2–5 and ª8–12, where he speaks of cases in which the faithfulness of the image is a necessary condition for successful remembering.

Admittedly, the word *eikôn* does not imply a very great degree of similarity, as we can see from Plato's discussions.[1] None the less, there is a limit. A moustache is not similar to a man, but rather (to cite one of the relations mentioned at 451^b19–20) is contiguous to him. Equally, an image that resembles a moustache is not similar to a man, and cannot reasonably be considered an *eikôn* of him. Nor will images that resemble an elephant, or an anvil, qualify as *eikones* of a man.

If this is so, how would Aristotle deal with images resembling a moustache, an elephant, or an anvil, when these represent a man? The materials for a theory are supplied by his account of the association of ideas in *De Memoria*, chapter 2. Borrowing from this account, someone might argue that, where it appears that we have only one image, and that it is a symbol for the man remembered without being an *eikôn* of him, the actual situation is that we have two images, both of them *eikones*. One is the image (and *eikôn*) of a moustache, elephant, or anvil. The other is the image (and *eikôn*) of the man himself. These two images are associated with each other. And immediately after having the image (and *eikôn*) of the moustache, we will have the image (and *eikôn*) of the man. This would be an interesting theory of symbolic images, and one which, if true, would protect Aristotle's theory, at least from the present line of criticism. But we are likely to protest that the copy of the man himself can be bypassed, and that the copy of the moustache is sufficient.

---

[1] The word is used by Plato when he calls time an *eikôn* of eternity (*Timaeus* 37D), when he speaks of ideal names and of some ordinary names as *eikones* of what they stand for (*Cratylus* 431D–433C; 439A–B), when he calls the words of poets *eikones* of what they portray (*Republic* 401B), when he speaks of analogies, such as that between a pilot or doctor and a ruler (*Statesman* 297E; cf. the references given by R. Robinson, in *Plato's Earlier Dialectic*, 2nd edition, London, 1954, p. 221: *Phaedo* 87B; *Republic* 375D; 487E; 509A; 517A–B; 538C), and when he describes things in the world as *eikones* of ideal Forms. Even for such Forms as Justice, Temperance and Wisdom, there are *eikones*, though not ones we can apprehend by sight (*Phaedrus* 250A–D). *Eikones* such as these can hardly resemble their originals very closely, and may be at best related as analogues to them. The *Cratylus* even points out that *eikones* have only some of the features of originals, or else they would be doubles. None the less, there is a limit. The *Cratylus*, which insists that an *eikôn* lacks some features of the original, also insists that it must be reasonably similar to the original. Not any name will be an *eikôn*, but only one in which most of the letters resemble what is being represented (433C). Again, the *Sophist* (235D–236C) appropriates the name '*eikôn*' for what is really similar, and not just apparently similar, to its original.

We can now confront the question why Aristotle postulates an image as involved in remembering. And we can add the related question why he postulates a copy or likeness.

One rather dull answer is that he is heavily influenced by Plato, or at least by one strand in Plato, which favours an image theory.[1] But this only raises the question why such a strand is to be found in Plato, and why Aristotle should have picked it out. In fact, until recent times, the most popular view has been that memory involves a mental or physical image.[2] Norman Malcolm has suggested some interesting reasons why the view should have appealed to various

---

[1] Plato's writings already contain the idea that memory and imagination involve the seeing of internal pictures (*Philebus* 38E–39D; *Phaedo* 73D; *Timaeus* 26D). Plato also postulates, but in a more light-hearted spirit than Aristotle, that memory involves a sort of imprint (*Theaetetus* 191C–196C; cf. *Timaeus* 71B for the case of dreams). And he explains by reference to the texture, consistency and size of what receives the imprint why some people remember better than others, and why it is not the same people who are good at learning and at remembering. There are many verbal echoes. Thus in the *Theaetetus*, we find talk of *daktulia* (signet rings, 191D; 193B–C), *apotupousthai* (to imprint, 191D), *ensêmainomenoi* (marking in, 191D); *sêmaia* (marks, 191D; 193B–C; 194C–195A). In the *Philebus* we find reference to a *zôgraphos* (a painter, 39B), and to *eikones* (copies, 39B–C). And the *Timaeus* talks of a *tupos* (imprint, 71B). These words, or their cognates, all appear in Aristotle's text. The notion of an *eikôn* also plays a part in Plato's various accounts of how we recollect the Forms, which we apprehended before birth. In many cases, we are reminded through encountering an *eikôn* of these Forms (see Norman Gulley, 'Plato's Theory of Recollection', *Classical Quarterly*, 1954), even though dialectical thought about the Forms rises above the need for *eikones*.

[2] Some people have followed the *Theaetetus*' simile of the block of wax, and have thought of memory as involving an imprint. They are then likely to think of the imprint as a mental or physical image. Others have followed the *Theaetetus*' simile of the aviary, and have thought of memory as a storehouse. They may then allow, as St. Augustine does, that only some of the things stored are images. Thoughts can be stored without the mediation of an image (*Confessions* X. 8–17). Recently, image theories of memory have come under repeated attack, but until recently, such attacks were rare. There is a striking attack by Plotinus on the idea that memory involves an imprint in the soul (*Enneads* IV. 6. I owe the reference to Malcolm Schofield; cf. IV. 3. 26 and 30). And Thomas Reid launched a powerful attack on image theories in *Essays on the Intellectual Powers of Man*, 1785, ed. Woozley, London, 1941, Essay III, and pp. xxvi, 233, 251. As an alternative to image theories, Samuel Alexander suggested a naïve realist view, according to which the object remembered is itself 'before my mind' and 'compresent with me' (*Space, Time and Deity*, London, 1920, vol. I, pp. 113–17).

modern philosophers.[1] I believe we can find in Aristotle a somewhat different set of reasons.

(a) First, why does he think that any kind of image is necessary? If we turn briefly from his theory of remembering to his theory of thinking, we can find a major reason why an image theory should have commended itself in this sphere. He holds that all human thinking requires images (DM 449^{b}31; DA 431^{a}16; 431^{b}2; 432^{a}8; ^{a}13). In this, he is no longer agreeing with Plato, but departing from him. For according to Plato, dialectical thinking rises above the need for images (Republic 510B; 511C; 532A). A reason for Aristotle's departure emerges at DA 432^{a}3–9. Objects of thought must be housed somewhere. Plato had supposed that the objects of dialectical thought were ideal Forms, which exist separately from the sensible world. But Aristotle believes that very few things can exist separately from the sensible world. So objects of thought need a sensible vehicle. And a convenient vehicle is the sensible form, which exists in external physical objects, and which during perception is transferred to one's sense-organs. An example of such a sensible form would be the colours of the external objects, colours which are taken on by one's eye-jelly during perception. These colours, first in the external object, then in the eye-jelly, provide a vehicle for the object of thought. And after perception is over, it is the resulting image that provides the vehicle.

Aristotle uses his view that thinking requires an image, in arguing for the idea that memory requires an image (see note on 450^{a}9–14, steps (ii) and (viii)).

(b) This may give us a hint why some kind of image is thought to be necessary. But it does not yet explain why a copy or likeness should be postulated. Here the theory of thinking can help us again, if we consider the kind of process that, according to Aristotle, is involved in thinking. The object of thought is within one's image (DA 431^{b}2). And in some cases one gets at it by attending to some features of one's image, and neglecting others (DM 450^{a}1–7).[2] For example, if one wishes to think of triangles, one will put before one's mind a triangle of a particular size, but neglect the irrelevant fact

[1] In 'Memory and Representation', Nous, 1970. In an earlier draft, Malcolm cited as examples Hume, James Mill, William James, Russell, Woozley, Stout, and (at one period) H. H. Price.

[2] Compare Berkeley, A Treatise Concerning the Principles of Human Knowledge, Introduction xvi.

that this particular imaged triangle happens to be, say, three inches across. If this is the kind of process involved in thinking about triangles, it is obvious that an image that is like a triangle will lend itself to the process, while an image that resembles one's geometry teacher, will not. For this reason, in thinking of triangles, one needs not merely an image, but an image that is to some extent *like* what one is thinking of.

(*c*) Another thought-process is described at *DM* 452^{b}7–15. Here one thinks of certain magnitudes by means of small-scale models in one's mind. For this thought-process too, not any kind of image will do, but only one that has the right proportions to act as a small-scale model. At this point, the theory of thinking directly influences the theory of remembering. For (452^{b}15–453^{a}4) when one remembers an event, and remembers how long ago it was, then too one makes use of images which are small-scale models. These images serve as a source of information about the length of time that has elapsed. And if they were not *eikones*, and did not preserve the right proportions, they could not perform this function. An impressionistic image of David and Goliath would not serve the purpose.

(*d*) Aristotle distinguishes between the image representing the time-lapse and the image representing the thing remembered. The latter serves as a reminder, if we are right in so translating *mnêmoneuma* at 450^{b}27 and 451^{a}2. It reminds one of or about the thing one is remembering. An image that was a copy of that thing would presumably perform this function particularly well.

(*e*) These considerations help to show why memory is supposed to involve a copy or likeness of the thing remembered and of the time elapsed. That the memory image would have to be a likeness, if not of the thing remembered, at any rate of something, follows from two Aristotelian considerations. First, if the image were not a likeness, it would not be an image *of* anything. And secondly, if we could not regard it as a likeness, then we could not have memory of something absent. We could only contemplate the image itself, which is something present (450^{b}11–451^{a}16).

We have been speaking as if one's memory-image of a scene is a copy of that scene, on Aristotle's theory. But sometimes Aristotle seems to imply the stronger view that the memory-image is a copy of *one's view of* that scene.[1]

---

[1] This was pointed out to me by Professor Anscombe. On the one hand, 450^{b}31 speaks of regarding one's image as being of the man, Coriscus. This

The preceding remarks have brought out in passing that the *De Memoria* is an important source for Aristotle's theory of thinking. It supplements the obscure and difficult account of the *De Anima*. We have argued that it helps to show why all human thinking is supposed to involve an image that is a likeness. *DM* 449^{b}30–450^{a}7 may also suggest a sense for the claim that the triangle which is the object of thought is *in*, or is *thought in*, an image (*DA* 431^{b}2; cf. 432^{a}4–5). And if we see in what way the object of thought is in, or is thought in, the image, this may help us to understand the claims that it is *in the soul*, and is *received*, and (harder still) the claim that, as fully actualized in the soul, it is numerically *identical* with the act of thinking. But to discuss these claims would involve us in too much speculation, and take us too far from the *De Memoria*.

The present state

We should now return to the question of what the present state consists in when one remembers. We have seen that the answer of Aristotle, and of many others, is that a major component of the present state is a mental image.[1] But the correct answer surely is[2] that the present state may consist in any of a great variety of things. It may involve an image. But it may involve simply thinking over, or recounting, or re-enacting a childhood scene without imagery. It may involve merely finding something familiar when one sees it, or feeding the cat, when one remembers to feed the cat, or striding over a missing step in the dark, when one remembers the missing step.[3]

(especially in conjunction with 451^{a}15–16) might lead one to think that the image is, on Aristotle's theory, simply a copy of Coriscus, not necessarily a copy of one's view of him. But 451^{a}4 speaks as if a memory-image needs to be in accordance, not merely with a past object of perception, but with the past perceiving of it. And again the quasi-imprint that is stamped into one is described as an imprint not of the sense-object, but of one's sense-image (*aisthêma* 450^{a}31–2).

[1] A number of philosophers more cautiously say that at any rate *true* or *genuine* memory involves a mental image, even if not all memory does.

[2] As has also been argued by Malcolm (*loc. cit.*), by Ayer (*The Problem of Knowledge*, Harmondsworth, 1956, ch. 4), and by Ryle (*The Concept of Mind*, London, 1949, ch. 8, sec. 7).

[3] In the last three examples, not only is a mental image absent, but it cannot even be said that any 'representation' (Martin and Deutscher, 'Remembering', *The Philosophical Review*, 1966) occurs. The example of remembering to feed the cat does not fit easily under the headings into which memory is most commonly divided (e.g. remembering that, remembering how to, remembering persons, things, or events). Consequently, it tends to be ignored in the literature.

Some of these examples, however, could not have occurred to Aristotle. For one thing, the case of finding something familiar when one sees it would not have been classed by him as a case of remembering, but only as a case of recognizing (*anagnôrizein*). For another thing, he would not admit the possibility of thinking over or recounting a scene without imagery, since in his view all thought and speech involves imagery.

What links the present state to something else?

There has been a long-standing question as to what links the present state of one who is remembering to something else, and to one particular thing (the thing remembered) rather than another. One version of this question asks what makes the memory-image to be an image *of* something. We have already noted Aristotle's answer to this. The image is *of* something by being a likeness or copy of that thing.

In explicit form, he raises only one question about linkage, and offers as the answer only one solution. The question explicitly raised is: how can perception of an image, which is present, yield memory of something which is absent (450^{b}11–20)? The answer is (450^{b}20–451^{a}16) that just as one can view a picture as a thing in its own right, or as a picture *of* something, so one can regard an image as a thing in its own right, or as being *of*, i.e. as being a copy of, something. The latter is what one does when remembering. With this one may compare William James' talk of referring one's image to the past (*The Principles of Psychology*, 1890, vol. I, p. 650).

A somewhat similar link is provided at an earlier point in the treatise, though it is not presented as an answer to the explicitly raised question. Aristotle says that, when remembering, one says in one's soul that one encountered this thing (i.e. the thing imaged) before.[1] Here too Aristotle's view, or something very like it, has been maintained by subsequent philosophers (James Mill, *Analysis of the Phenomena of the Human Mind* [1st edition 1829] new edition 1869, vol. I, pp. 328–31; John Locke, *An Essay Concerning Human Understanding*, book II, chapter X, sec. 2; William James, *op. cit.*, pp. 648–652; Russell, *The Analysis of Mind*, 1921, pp. 160, 170, 179).

---

[1] 449^{b}22–3. Cf. also 450^{a}19–21, if we are right in emending the latter to read *proteron prosaisthanetai*, and translating, '. . . when someone is actively engaged in memory, he perceives in addition that he saw this, or heard it, or learned it earlier'.

Unfortunately, it is rather hard to square this last requirement with Aristotle's claim (450ᵃ15–16) that memory can belong to animals which lack judgment and intelligence. Can they say anything in their souls? Moreover, both of the last two requirements create difficulty for him, when he goes on to consider the case of a man who is in doubt whether he is remembering (451ᵃ2–5). Apparently, this doubt is due to his being unsure whether his image is 'in accordance with' a previous perception. Apparently also the doubt takes the form of wondering whether he should regard his image as a copy. In view of this, the doubter may well refrain in many cases from regarding his image as a copy, and from saying in his soul that he encountered the imaged thing before. In these cases, given Aristotle's requirements for remembering, the doubt will supply its own answer. For the doubter fails to meet two of Aristotle's requirements, and so cannot be remembering. At the same time, by simply setting his doubts aside, he can, provided the other conditions are fulfilled, meet all Aristotle's requirements for remembering. These surprising consequences call into question Aristotle's idea that one who remembers must regard his image as a copy, and must say in his soul that he encountered something before.

There are other difficulties also in Aristotle's two suggestions about linkage.[1] Some difficulties are avoided by the suggestion[2] that the link between one's present state and the past is a causal one. The most persuasive causal account is one which says that, in remembering, one's present state (which does not always involve an image) is causally related to a past act of cognition (which is not always a perceptual one). One does not have to agree with the

---

[1] Rather similar to the case of being uncertain whether one is remembering is the case of being quite unaware that one is. Martin and Deutscher (*op. cit.*, pp. 166–8) have argued convincingly that this is compatible with remembering.

Another difficulty is that of explaining without a regress what it is to regard one's image as a copy of, say, the man, Coriscus. Does this involve thinking of Coriscus, and connecting one's memory-image with him? If so, a question would arise as to how one thinks of the absent Coriscus. And this is unfortunately as hard, or as easy, to answer as the original question of how one *remembers* the absent Coriscus.

Finally, there is the possibility of regarding one's image as a copy, or not a copy, and of saying things in one's soul, merely by way of experiment, when one is in doubt whether one is remembering, or merely as a feat of imagination, or merely on the basis of evidence. It is hard to believe that doing this can make all the difference between remembering and not remembering.

[2] Martin and Deutscher (*loc. cit.*).

further suggestion[1] that the causal link takes the form of a physical trace, or structural analogue, in order to accept the general idea that there must be some causal link or other. Aristotle postulates a causal link, namely a sort of physical imprint, that connects one's present mental image with an earlier act of perception, though he does not offer this as the answer to the question he explicitly raises about linkage.

But for the causal link, one's image would not be a copy of something. The other implication of its being a copy is that it is to some extent like that of which it is a copy. The requirements of a causal connexion and of likeness[2] provide two distinguishable links. We have seen (p. 3, n. 1) that there are cases where memory does depend on one's having an image that is reasonably like the thing remembered. The mistake of supposing that memory requires this in all cases has been shared by many philosophers.[3]

Memory images and other images

There has been another long-standing problem for accounts of memory, namely how to distinguish between memory and other states of mind. The question is particularly acute for theories that make remembering, perceiving and imagining[4] all to be forms of imaging. For Aristotle, memory-images are not identical with sense-images (*aisthêmata*), but are produced from them by a kind of imprinting process (*DM* 450ª30–2). In a similar way, Hume sometimes declares impressions to be the causes of ideas (*A Treatise of Human Nature* 1.1.1).

But Aristotle does not make the mistake of supposing that memory can be distinguished from perception or imagination simply by reference to the character of the images involved. To discover the differences, one needs to read the full account of perception and of

[1] Introduced by Martin and Deutscher for a separate purpose.

[2] For the requirement of likeness, note the following. The image must be a copy (450ᵇ27; 451ª2; ª11–12), and must be in accordance with a past perception (451ª4). If one is in doubt or mistaken in thinking that this condition is met, then one is in doubt or mistaken in supposing one remembers (451ª2–5; 451ª10–12; 452ᵇ24–6).

[3] For documentation, see Malcolm, *loc. cit.*

[4] For attempts to distinguish between memory and imagination, see Hobbes, *Leviathan*, chapter 2; Hume, *A Treatise of Human Nature*, book I, part I, sec. III; book I, part III, sec. V; Russell, *op. cit.*, p. 176; James Mill, *op. cit.*, pp. 328–331; William James, *op. cit.*, p. 652.

imagination in the *De Anima* (*DA* II.6–III.2, and III.3), and compare it with the account of memory here.[1]

A further problem is created by the enormous variety of images there are. The variety includes the diverse kinds of after-image, the so-called eidetic images,[2] and images of the kind reported by the mnemonist Shereshevskii.[3] These are all different from each other, and the first group at least is not naturally counted as a species of memory-image. But how is it to be distinguished? Aristotle's answer is clear. He counts after-images as *aisthêmata* (sense-images *Insom.* 460b2–3). They therefore differ from memory-images in their causal history.[4]

Remembering and relearning

Another distinction that has proved difficult to draw is that between remembering something learnt and learning it again for a second time.[5] Aristotle discusses the related problem (see pp. 37–40) of how to distinguish between recollecting and relearning. He does not explicitly discuss the distinction between remembering and relearning. But he supplies plenty of materials for an answer. For example, he would claim that cases of relearning lack the very special causal link that he ascribes to memory, a link involving the persistence of a sort of imprint within one. This quasi-imprint is like the trace to which Martin and Deutscher appeal (*op. cit.*, pp. 189–91), in order to deal with the closely related problem of when a man, who has been put into a suggestible state by witnessing some

---

[1] Among the characteristics of memory which help to distinguish it from imagination, Aristotle might name the (correct) judgment that one encountered the imaged thing before, the attitude of regarding one's image as a copy, and the co-presence of a mental image revealing the time elapsed. He would also require that the image be a true copy of something.

[2] See R. N. Haber, 'Eidetic Images', *Scientific American*, 1969; G. W. Allport, 'Eidetic Imagery', *British Journal of Psychology*, 1924.

[3] A. R. Luria, *The Mind of a Mnemonist*, London and New York, 1969, esp. p. 62.

[4] Not only are memory-images imprints produced from *aisthêmata*. But even when they've been produced, a person cannot be said to have memory until a little time has elapsed (*DM* 451a25–31). Aristotle also takes note of various features of after-images, by reference to which psychologists classify them. They may require a long fixation period (*Insom.* 459b11). They can follow the direction of one's gaze (459b11–13; b18–20). Some start the same colour as the object one was looking at (459b12; b16), but thereafter change colour (459b16–18).

[5] See the detailed discussion by Martin and Deutscher, *loc. cit.*

events, is genuinely remembering the events on being told of them, and when he is only doing something else, such as learning about them again. Just as Martin and Deutscher's trace is a structural analogue of what is remembered, so Aristotle's quasi-imprint is like a picture (450ᵃ29–30; ᵇ16).

Is memory of the past?

Aristotle says (449ᵇ10–15) that the object of memory is the past (or, perhaps, what is past). This view is understandable and is widely shared.[1] But in fact there are many cases where it is not at all clear that the view is true. For example, one can remember a fact, how to do something, a number which one has memorized, the flavour of honey, to feed the cat, the way from A to B, the strokes in swimming, the Queen's presence, tomorrow's appointment or meeting, a character in fiction, the incommensurability of the diagonal and the side of a square.

It may be thought that these cases are exceptions which can be relegated to certain special categories of memory. And it is true that a good many of the examples can be relegated to the categories of remembering that something is the case, or remembering how to do something. But this still leaves an awkward residue. It may be thought that at least there is a *type* of memory of which the view is true. And perhaps there is. But if so, it is important to be able to spell out what the type is. And this is not so easy a task as one might suppose.

For present purposes, it is enough to say that at least Aristotle is not in a position to defend his view that the thing remembered belongs to the past. For in several of the examples which he actually discusses, and which were listed above (p. 1), the view is not true.

Perhaps the correct view is that memory involves past cognition of a thing, if we may use the word 'cognition' to cover learning, learning of, perceiving, thinking of, reading about, being told, knowing, feeling, etc. The past cognition is normally of the thing subsequently remembered. For example, one cognizes that it is midnight, and subsequently remembers that it was midnight. (It is only by a sort of extension that one sometimes talks of remembering

---

[1] For antecedents, see Plato, *Philebus* 39D. Reid (*op. cit.*, Essay III), Russell (*op. cit.*, pp. 167, 176, 179, 186), and Martin and Deutscher (*op. cit.*, p. 166) assume, at least in connexion with the kind of memory on which they are concentrating, that the thing remembered will in every case be past.

that it is long after midnight, where what one previously cognized was its being midnight, not its being long after.)

A great advantage of accepting the past-cognition view is that it enables one to explain why the past-object view was so tempting. In many cases, cognition and thing cognized are contemporary with each other. In all these cases, if the cognition is past, as it is when one remembers something, the thing cognized, and hence the thing subsequently remembered, will also have existed in the past.

The mental image and the physical trace

What is the relation, in Aristotle's account, of the mental image to the physical trace? He does not seem to keep them sharply distinct. Through most of 450ª25–451ª17, we have every reason to think he is discussing what we should call a mental image. Thus he calls the image a *phantasma* (450ᵇ10; ᵇ24; ᵇ26; ᵇ29; 451ª10;ª15). He says that the image is 'in the soul' (450ª28; ᵇ10–11; 451ª3).[1] We may also be struck by the statement that the man who is remembering perceives and contemplates the image within him (450ᵇ15–18; 450ᵇ24–451ª2).[2] How could such an image, we may wonder, be a merely physical imprint? Must he not be talking of a mental image?

Interpretation is complicated by the fact that Aristotle seems to interchange talk of a *phantasma*, of a certain picture-like effect (*zôgraphêma, graphê, zôon*), and of a certain quasi-imprint (*tupos*). These equations become apparent gradually. At 450ª30 it is the picture-like effect, but at 451ª14–16 it is the *phantasma*, the having of which is said to be memory. Next, it appears that this same picture-like effect is identical with the quasi-imprint. This is suggested, at any rate, by the fact that at 450ª31 the notion of an imprint is meant to explain why the effect in question is like a picture. And at 450ᵇ16 the quasi-imprint and the picture-like effect are explicitly equated. Finally, in 450ᵇ20–451ª2 the *phantasma* is treated as picture-like.

These equations on their own create no difficulty. But problems begin in 450ª30–ᵇ10, where the quasi-imprint is given a very

[1] The expression 'a process *of* the soul' would be less significant, since it applies to such non-mental processes as the growth of a plant. But the expression used here is '*in* the soul'.

[2] Though here we should recall that, in Aristotle's view, one can perceive processes within one that are merely physiological. For example, a person who is seeing is sometimes said to perceive the coloration of his own eye-jelly (*DS* 447ª23–7; *GA* 780ᵇ32; *DA* 425ᵇ19; ᵇ22–3).

physical interpretation. The surfaces within the body, it is said, must not be too hard to receive it. Does this mean that the mental image is also being regarded as a physical affection?

Things will fall into place, if we call to mind Aristotle's theory in *DA* 403ᵃ3–ᵇ19 (compare *DS* 436ᵃ6–10, which explicitly mentions memory). He has no word, nor even any concept, corresponding to our 'mental'. But none the less, he does not say of what we should call mental affections that they are simply physiological processes. He allows that in some sense of 'is' anger, or smelling, *is* a physiological process. And in an analogous sense a house *is* bricks. But he considers it is entirely misleading to say that a house is 'simply' bricks, or that anger and smelling are 'simply' physiological processes. A house is also a shelter (403ᵇ3–9), anger is also a desire to retaliate (403ᵃ25–ᵇ3), and smelling is also an awareness of odour (*aisthanesthai*, 424ᵇ17–19).¹ If he has any hesitation at all, it is about saying that a house is bricks, and in general that a thing is its matter (*Metaph.* 1035ᵃ7–10; 1041ᵇ12–16). He does not hesitate to say that a house is its form—a shelter.

We should not suppose that desire and awareness are extra components in anger and smelling. A shelter is not a component in a house. It is rather that the descriptions 'desire' and 'awareness' supply very important information, which is not given in the talk of physiological processes, and which cannot be neglected. In saying this, Aristotle is exploiting our intuition that desire and awareness are themselves not simply physiological processes. We may wish that he had explained why they are not, by finding for desire and awareness descriptions of a different kind, which do not to the same extent invite the question: 'And why are those not simply physiological processes?' We can only guess what descriptions he might have been willing to offer.² But it is at least clear that for him neither anger nor desire, neither smelling nor awareness, are simply physiological processes.

Applying this to the memory image, we can see that Aristotle would not have the concepts for characterizing this as mental. But

---

¹ Aristotle is at least as ready to say that a mental affection *is* a certain formal cause, as to say that it *is* a certain material cause. Thus it *is* an enmattered form (403ᵃ25), just as a house *is* a form (403ᵇ6). Again anger *is* a movement of a faculty (desire?), as well as being a physiological movement (403ᵃ26–7).

² Would he have been willing to say, for example, that desire has an end, and is an efficient cause of action towards that end?

none the less, he would deny that the image was 'simply' physiological. The memory image is a physiological affection, in some sense of 'is' analogous to that in which a house is bricks. But it is not 'simply' this.

A further question about the relation of mental image and physical affection is whether both have actual existence continuously, or whether, as one would expect, the mental image comes into existence only from time to time. The latter is suggested by the talk of certain images occurring simultaneously when one performs an act of remembering, as if they came into actual existence then (452^b23-4). It is also suggested by the talk of changes occurring in succession, following each other, and being undergone, when one is recollecting ($451^b10-452^a16$). On the other hand, Aristotle describes these same changes or images as being 'possessed' (450^a30; 451^a16; 452^a11-12), which suggests something less intermittent, and he talks of them as 'remaining' in the soul (450^b10-11; 453^b2-3), as if they were something permanent. Presumably, the continuous existence which he attributes to the mental image is a merely potential existence, the potential existence which is supplied by the continued actual existence of the physical trace.

The view that the mental image is, among other things, a physiological entity, and the corresponding view of DA 403^a26; $^a31-^b1$ that anger is, among other things, an obscure physiological process such as might be discovered by scientists, may seem surprising to some contemporary ears. At any rate, a stir was caused when it was suggested in a number of recent publications that sensations might yet turn out to *be* brain processes. A whole literature has grown up on this subject, and several anthologies have now been devoted to it.[1] However, in the case of Aristotle what is remarkable is that he should be beginning to break away from this kind of idea. His analogy of a house and bricks is very close to some of the analogies in recent literature. But he is unlike many recent contributors, when he insists that a house is not 'simply' bricks. And he is also unlike them in that he will not talk of identity (*to auto*), and say that a house is *identical* with a set of bricks (cf. *Metaph.* 1041^b13). This is noteworthy, because there were influences that might well

[1] John O'Connor (ed.), *Modern Materialism: Readings on Mind-Body Identity*, New York, 1969; C. V. Borst (ed.), *The Mind-Brain Identity Theory*, London, 1970; C. F. Presley (ed.), *The Identity Theory of Mind*, St. Lucia, Queensland, 1967.

have led him to take the simpler materialistic view. For one thing, many of Aristotle's predecessors were preoccupied with the physiological side of mental occurrences. Many of their statements, at least if taken in isolation, as Aristotle often took them, could suggest a simple identification of some mental occurrence with some physiological thing. And Aristotle, along with his successor Theophrastus, and later commentators who drew on Theophrastus, seem often to have interpreted early writers in this sense.[1]

Aristotle might also have been led to the simpler materialist view by his conception of the soul according to which the biological process of growth is on a level with conscious activity. Both are equally due to the soul. In fact, however, instead of declaring that conscious activity is therefore 'simply' a physical process he prefers to deny that biological growth is 'simply' a physical process—which is not however to say that it is a mental one. Growth is also a development towards an end. And desire, perhaps, is an efficient cause of action towards an end.

There are many passages where Aristotle does speak of a mental affection in physical terms. And his treatment of the memory image here is a case in point. But for a full understanding, these statements need to be read in the light of the more explicit theoretical statements quoted from the *De Anima*.[2] His view does not fit neatly in with present-day ways of thought. He is not like contemporary materialists. Nor on the other hand does he postulate a Cartesian act of mind.

[1] See *Metaph.* 1009ᵇ11ff on Empedocles and Democritus. See also Parmenides, fragment 6, lines 5–6; fragment 16, in Diels, *Die Fragmente der Vorsokratiker*. Empedocles, fragment 105, Diels. Anaxagoras, according to Theophrastus, *De Sensibus*, Sec. 31. Democritus, according to Aëtius, A30 in Diels. Some of Plato's *Timaeus* also lends itself to this kind of interpretation. On Homer, see R. B. Onians, *The Origins of European Thought*, 2nd edition, Cambridge, 1953. For Aristotle's interpretation of some earlier views on pleasure (those of Plato in the *Philebus*? of Speusippus? of Aristippus?), see *NE* 1173ᵇ7–9.

[2] The fullest recent statement ascribing a materialist position to Aristotle is that of T. Slakey, 'Aristotle on Sense Perception', *The Philosophical Review*, 1961. However, Slakey rests his case mainly on a construction of *DA* 423ᵇ27–424ᵃ10, which cannot, I think, be supported. For another materialist interpretation, see Wallace I. Matson, 'Why Isn't the Mind-Body Problem Ancient?' in *Mind, Matter and Method*, edd. Feyerabend and Maxwell, University of Minnesota, 1966. I have discussed the whole subject of this section, and have offered substantiation for the views here expressed, in 'Body and Soul in Aristotle,' forthcoming.

Dating a past event

How do we tell when a remembered event occurred? Russell suggests that we may have a succession of images, or a whole set of images co-present, but fading in such a way that they can be placed in a series (*op. cit.*, p. 162).[1] Few people, when reflecting on their own experience, will find it plausible that they undergo such imagery. Yet once one makes the mistake of supposing that one has to tell the date of a remembered event from some feature of one's present experience, one is forced into postulating such implausible mechanisms as this.

The mechanism that Aristotle postulates is not more implausible than Russell's, though it may be more ingenious. He claims that one tells the date of a remembered event from a mental image. The image takes the form of a diagram, which may look like this.

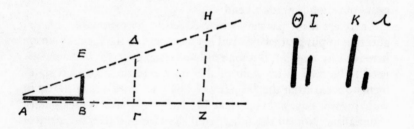

This is a version of the diagram that was reconstructed from Aristotle's text by J. I. Beare and W. D. Ross, working independently. The continuous lines represent those parts of the mental diagram that are given. The broken lines represent those parts that one constructs.

Aristotle begins (452^b8-15) by comparing the technique to that involved in thinking about spatial magnitudes. It soon emerges that he means thinking about the *relative* sizes of two or more objects, not thinking about the absolute size of a single object. One thinks about the relative sizes of two or more objects by having images which serve as small-scale models. The larger image corresponds to the larger object and the smaller to the smaller. We might expect then that Aristotle will discuss how to estimate the relative lengths

[1] Compare James Mill, *op. cit.*, I, 330–1; Hume, *op. cit.*, II.III.VII.

of two time periods. And sure enough, when he introduces the mental diagram for judging time-lapses (452^b15–22) we find that there are two time periods involved, one corresponding to AB, and one to BE, in the mental diagram. The reason for supposing that he has in mind two time periods, not one, is that the mental diagram has more parts than would be needed for dealing with a single time period.

But why does he introduce two time periods? For surely we only need to know about one, the time-lapse since the remembered event. One possibility is that he envisages a person who is dating one event relatively to another. The relative lengths of AB and BE show him how much longer ago one event occurred than the other. Alternatively, W. D. Ross may be right in suggesting that AB is used for estimating how long ago the event started, BE for estimating its duration. (There will then be no use for BE, if what is remembered is a fact, a person, etc.)

But still, even if we are interested in two time periods, we are likely to want to know more about them than their relative lengths. We shall probably want to know their absolute lengths. Or at least we shall want to know the absolute length of one, from which, together with the relative lengths, we can calculate the absolute length of the other. Now if Aristotle had only wanted to show us how to estimate the relative lengths, he would have left us with a simpler diagram, containing only AB and BE. The relative lengths of these would reveal the relative lengths of the two time periods. In fact, however, he includes a lot more apparatus in the diagram. It is presumably meant to show how we can estimate the absolute length of the time periods. How is this to be done?

We start by being given certain lines, namely AB, BE, Θ and I. These lines are given in that they simply appear before the mind's eye, presumably because there are corresponding lines physically imprinted in one's central sense-organ. (No doubt, if these lines are to continue giving accurate information in the future, they will have slowly to alter their lengths appropriately, as time passes.)

Having been given these lines, we are to construct others, namely AΓ and ΓΔ. These, though larger respectively than AB and BE, are to bear the same ratio to each other. One way of ensuring that they do preserve this ratio is to make ΓΔ parallel to BE, thus obtaining similar triangles (ABE and AΓΔ).

How much larger should one make the constructed lines, AΓ and

ΓΔ, than the given ones, AB and BE? This is revealed by the lines Θ and I, lines which are also given from the start. As Θ exceeds I in length, so must AΓ exceed AB (and so must ΓΔ exceed BE, but this will be achieved automatically, if one makes ΓΔ parallel to BE).

If instead of Θ and I, one is given K and Λ, then one will construct a pair of lines which are larger yet (though they still bear the same ratio to each other), namely AZ and ZH.

If instead of starting with AB, BE, one had started with a pair of lines bearing a different ratio to each other, then the constructed lines would have borne a different ratio to each other.

But this does not yet tell us how to estimate the absolute length of any time period. For the mental diagram is entirely spatial in character. How can one move from a purely spatial diagram to a conclusion about the absolute length of some time period? Perhaps Aristotle would answer[1] that one does not statically view the imaged diagram, but moves in one's mind along the lines that compose it at a standard pace determined by human physiology. From the short time-span that is required for the mental movement along the line BE, one can calculate the greater time-span which one is seeking. Thus one is relying not on the length of the line BE, but on the time required to traverse it mentally.[2] Once one has calculated one of the two time periods, one can rapidly calculate the other, through knowledge of the relative lengths.

But this solution would raise in turn a further problem. When the mental movement along the line BE terminates, how can one know what its duration has been? Must one rely on memory? Must one appeal to yet another mental diagram? In either case, the account would be threatened with a regress. No doubt, Aristotle would say it cannot be through memory that one estimates the short

[1] Another solution would be to say that the lines, AB, BE, represent durations, perhaps the duration of the sequence of images we have while thinking back to the start of the remembered event, and the duration of the sequence of images we have while mentally running over the event. From the first duration we estimate how long ago the event started, from the second how long it lasted. This suggestion is in many ways attractive, though it does not seem to fit very easily with lines 452^{b}23–9, which suggest that the imagery that reveals the time may occur without the image of the remembered event, and *vice versa*. I owe the idea of this solution to Mr. Richard Hawkins, though he would not accept the use to which the idea is put.

[2] Indeed, when Aristotle speaks of the *kinêsis* BE, he may mean not the *change* BE (i.e. the image, or image-fragment, BE), but the *motion* BE (i.e. the motion from B to E along that image-fragment).

term duration, since (451^a29–31) one cannot yet remember what is only just past (a view shared by those who postulate a specious present). But how then does one estimate it? Can it be through sense-perception? Certainly, Aristotle thinks that motion, change, and the passage of time can be objects of perception (DA 425^a16; $Phys.$ 219^a3–4; see also note on DM 449^b29).

The specious present has been invoked by some philosophers for the apprehension of motion, change, and the passage of time, and for the estimation of time-spans. According to William James (*op. cit.*, pp. 605–48), the specious present is a period of less than a minute, which culminates in the present instant, and the whole of which can be before the mind at the present instant. Neither the events contained in the specious present, nor the apparent duration of it, are presented to us through memory. It is a sensation that gives us its apparent duration (pp. 632–42). It is not clear that Aristotle ever postulates a specious present.[1] But might he none the less, in the same spirit as William James, suggest that it is a sensation which reveals the duration of the mental movement along BE?

James' account is related to Aristotle's in yet another way. For James goes on (p. 638) to treat the apparent duration of the specious present rather as Aristotle treats his small-scale mental diagram. From this apparent duration, according to James, one acquires a sense of the greater duration that separates a past event from the present instant. As is the number of events intervening since that past event to the number of experiences contained in the specious present, so we suppose is the duration intervening since that past event to the duration of the specious present.

Retrospect

In a recent study (*A Portrait of Aristotle*, London, 1963, chapter five), Marjorie Grene has drawn a sharp contrast between Aristotle's account of memory and the empiricist theory of Hume. The present Chapter and Chapter 3 below suggest that Aristotle avoided raising some of the empiricists' questions, and avoided some of the excesses in their answers, but that none the less his account is close in many ways to theirs.

---

[1] The nearest he comes to postulating a specious present is perhaps in 451^a29–31 (see note). He there speaks as if, at any given instant, the present has a certain span, and includes within itself experiences which one has just had.

2. Mnemonic Techniques

The place system

The most famous of the techniques for remembering developed in ancient Greece is the so-called place system. Aristotle mentions it four times.[1] The only extant ancient descriptions are Roman ones.[2] There may well have been other varieties of it than the one described in the three Roman texts. But on the other hand, the name 'places' is not a name for any kind of mnemonic system. It covers only systems that have something to do with places. What this involves will become clearer as we go along.

Considerable claims were made on behalf of this or similar systems. Quintilian suggests that the place system may have been used by the man who could watch a full day's auction, and at the end of the day name all the articles sold, the buyers and the prices.[3] It is often assumed by commentators, though without explicit textual evidence, that it was the place system which Hippias and Seneca used.[4] Hippias is made to boast in Plato's *Hippias Major* that he has a technique for repeating fifty names after a single hearing.[5] And Seneca, father of the philosopher, claims that he was once able to repeat two thousand names after a single hearing, or two hundred disconnected lines of verse shouted out to him by members of his audience. And he could repeat the lines either in the order given, or in the reverse order.[6] In modern times, L. A. Post has described in the *Classical Weekly* the striking, if somewhat

---

[1] *Top.* 163ᵇ28; *DA* 427ᵇ18; *DM* 452ᵃ12-16; *Insom.* 458ᵇ20-2.

[2] In chronological order, the *Rhetorica ad Herennium* III.16-24; Cicero, *De Oratore* II.353-60; Quintilian, *Institutio Oratoria* XI.2.17-26.

[3] *Institutio Oratoria* XI.2.24.

[4] It is at any rate likely to have been some system involving mental images that they used. I. M. L. Hunter in *Memory*, Harmondsworth, revised edition, 1964, remarks (p. 213) that, so far as he knows, all those who are accomplished at memorizing large amounts of relatively meaningless material use imaging as a central part of their procedures. Similarly L. A. Post, 'Ancient Memory Systems', *Classical Weekly*, 1932, p. 105.

[5] *Hippias Major* 285E.

[6] *Controversiarum Libri*, Lib. I, Praef. 2.

less startling, results that he achieved by means of the place system.[1]

A technique surprisingly close to the place system has been described by the Soviet psychologist A. R. Luria, in *The Mind of a Mnemonist*.[2] Luria does not allude to the ancient place system. He simply describes the technique of a remarkable Russian mnemonist, Shereshevskii. Shereshevskii was not taught his technique. He possessed it as a natural gift, though he improved and elaborated it by training. He was able by means of it to repeat indefinitely long lists of items after a single hearing, and to repeat them again after an interval of fifteen, sixteen or twenty years. Luria never found a list so long that Shereshevskii could not repeat it perfectly. This does not of course mean that an ordinary person would be able to achieve such feats simply by mastering the place system. But if one reads Luria's account, one can understand the Roman accounts better, when one goes back to them.

How does the place system work?[3] In its Roman version, it involves forming two sets of images. First, one memorizes in advance a set of places, for example a street of houses, which will form background images. This is the laborious part of the method. The places must be firmly fixed in one's mind, by dint of picturing them to oneself in the right order over and over again. It does not matter whether the places one pictures are real or imaginary. Shereshevskii used Gorky Street in Moscow. Quintilian suggests using the rooms of a house.

Then comes the second stage of the procedure. Supposing one wishes to memorize the main points in a speech, one will form a second set of images symbolizing these points. The image symbolizing the first point will then be superimposed on the image of the first place, that symbolizing the second point on the image of the second place, and so on. When one wishes to recollect, one will run through the set of places in one's mind and find the superimposed images. One will not survey the entire set of places in a

---

[1] *Op. cit.*, pp. 105–10. For other ancient stories, see e.g. Seneca, *op. cit.*, Lib. I, Praef. 18–19; Quintilian, *op. cit.*, XI.2.22–6; Pliny, *Natural History* VII.24. For the tale of Simonides' supposed discovery of the system, in the sixth to fifth centuries B.C., see Quintilian, *op. cit.*, XI.2.11–16.

[2] *Op. cit.* Also in 'Memory and the Structure of Mental Processes', in *Problems of Psychology*, no. 1, Oxford, 1960.

[3] An excellent account is given by Frances Yates, in *The Art of Memory*, London, 1965.

single panorama, but rather will move in one's mind from one place to the next.

The same set of background places can subsequently be used for memorizing a different speech, or a poem, or a set of fifty names. Some of the Roman accounts compare the background places to a writing tablet, and the foreground images to letters written on the tablet. One can erase the letters, and will be able to use the same writing tablet again. Thus when one has once made the effort to fix a set of places in one's mind, one can use the same set of places any number of times.

But what is the point of having two sets of images? Wouldn't it be simpler to have just one? The use of two sets has a number of advantages. First, one will remember not only the points in one's speech, but also, thanks to the background places, their order.[1] Next, the background places can supply a connexion in cases where the items one is memorizing have no memorable connexion of their own. Then, a street of houses is something one can scan through very rapidly. Moreover, one can run through the street in either direction, and hence can recall the things memorized in the original, or in the reverse, order. This is an advantage mentioned in the *Rhetorica ad Herennium*,[2] and by Luria.[3] It also accounts, no doubt, for Seneca having been able to recite his two hundred unconnected lines of verse in reverse order. Again, as is pointed out by Luria,[4] and by Hunter in his book on memory,[5] it is very easy, while using a given place as one's base, to take a look at the places on either side, and so recall the memorized items on either side. Finally, with a little elaboration, the system permits one to skip over certain places, and visit, say, every fifth one. An elaboration of this kind is described in the *Rhetorica ad Herennium*.[6] In the fifth place, the author suggests, one should station the image of a golden hand with five fingers, and in the tenth place the image of a friend named Decimus ('Tenth'). We find already as early as Aristotle the suggestion that some use be made of numbers in connexion with a process that he explicitly compares with the process of using places. His students

[1] Cicero, *De Oratore* II, 353; 354; 359.
[2] *Ibid.*, III.17–18.
[3] *Op. cit.*, pp. 31–2.
[4] *Op. cit.*, pp. 32–3.
[5] *Memory*, Harmondsworth, revised edition, 1964, pp. 215–16.
[6] III.18.

are to be able to take a mental look at the patterns of argument they have memorized, classified according to numbers.[1]

Some of the advantages of the place-method can be obtained by using a simpler system of images.[2] But the place-method tends to be more efficient, and simpler systems often do not permit such refinements as landing, say, on every fifth item in the series, when one is recollecting.

Even with this description, it may seem puzzling how the place-method was able to achieve such good results, until one notes the very vivid character of the images that are formed, when the method is properly practised. Because of this, the process of recollecting is very like that of scanning a picture, or series of pictures. Luria describes the vivid and pictorial nature of Shereshevskii's images. If Shereshevskii made a mistake in recollecting, it was never due to a failure of retention, but to a perceptual failure in scrutinizing his images. His images of things needed to be well-lit. If they were not, he might have mentally to bring up a street lamp, so as to brighten his image of something. Foreground images needed to be contrasted with background ones. He had to avoid smoke or fog obscuring the view. His images of things had to be sufficiently large for him not to lose sight of them. And he tried to avoid imagining very crowded scenes, if some abbreviation could be substituted in place of the details. He described what he was doing in terms of 'spotting' things, or 'making things out'. And Luria reports that when he repeated a list of things, it was as if he had the list still in front of him, and was reading it through. If a 3 earlier presented to him had been badly written, he might subsequently 'misread' it as an 8.

Sir Francis Galton discovered, during his researches into mental images in the last century, that scientists and philosophers tended to have rather feeble images.[3] For those of us of whom this is true, it may take quite an effort to realize how very akin the process of recollecting by places is to the process of scanning pictures. Of course, we should not simply assume that what was true of one very unusual person, Shereshevskii, would be true of others. But, in fact,

[1] For further details on this, see below.

[2] Hunter, *op. cit.*, pp. 213-16, 297-8.

[3] (*Inquiries into Human Faculty*, London, 1883; 2nd edition, 1907.) I confess, however, to having number images of the kind he investigated, and to finding some of them bright and some of them dim.

Shereshevskii's account of his images is closely matched in the Roman discussions of place-memory.

The *Rhetorica ad Herennium* insists that the imaged places should be conspicuous, that they should not be crowded, that they should differ from each other, that they should be of moderate size, neither so large that the images superimposed on them will be vague, nor so small that an arrangement of images cannot be superimposed, that they should not be dimly lit, nor on the other hand too bright, that they should be spaced about thirty feet apart from each other, so that the background scenes will not appear too close, nor too far away.[1] Turning to the foreground images, the treatise recommends using abbreviated symbols, and insists that the images should be vivid and striking, not too numerous, nor too vague, but carefully delineated. The advice is very like that which Shereshevskii was later to formulate for himself, and it implies vivid, picture-like images.

A final puzzle is this. It is easy to see how the place system could be used for memorizing a dozen names. But how could it be used for memorizing two thousand? One possibility is that one could stack a series of images outside each front door in the street. The late Professor Durham of Cornell University used a method in which he hung several items, as it were, on each peg.[2] Another possibility is suggested by the claims of Peter of Ravenna, in the fifteenth century, whose method involved employing 100,000 places.[3] Whatever we think of this figure, it may be that some people can store a very large number of places. Quintilian mentions a particular set of 360 places that was used by Metrodorus.[4] And certainly the *Rhetorica ad Herennium* tells us flatly that, if we want to remember many things, we shall have to prepare many places.[5]

Dialectic and mnemonics

Now why should Aristotle have been interested in mnemonics? Not only does he mention the place system four times, but in the *De Memoria* he discusses mnemonics. And he is said by Diogenes Laertius to have written a work on the subject.

[1] If they were further apart, one would tend to view them as distant, so as to facilitate the transition from one to the next over the intervening ground.

[2] So I am told by Professor Gordon Kirkwood.

[3] *Artificiosa Memoria*, Venice, 1491, Fol. 102ᵛ.

[4] *Op. cit.*, XI.2.22

[5] III.17.

Discussion has centred on the role of memorizing in rhetoric. But Aristotle says much more about its importance for dialectic.[1] This aspect of the subject is less well known. Dialectical debating, as he taught it, was a development of the kind of debating that had been practised by Protagoras[2] and other sophists of the previous century. Socrates practises a version or versions of it in many of Plato's dialogues. And Aristotle gives his own instructions to students of it in the eighth book of the *Topics*.[3]

In the debates which Aristotle discusses, one person, the answerer, would be required to defend a certain thesis. His opponent, the questioner, would try to make him admit the negation of that thesis. He would do so by putting questions in a form that called for a 'yes' or 'no' answer. With certain exceptions, other forms of question and answer were not allowed.[4] There was a time limit set.[5] An audience would be present,[6] equipped to assess the quality of the arguing.[7] There were rules as to what was permitted and what was not. Against competitive or contentious people almost anything was permitted.[8] But Aristotle will not normally dignify the arguments in this kind of debating with the title 'dialectical'. He refers to them instead as 'competitive' or 'contentious'.[9] In genuine dialectic, the arguments must be valid, and not just seemingly valid.[10] And another important rule is that the questioner must argue from premises that are accepted, accepted, that is, by people in general,

---

[1] The bulk of the ancient evidence concerns the use of mnemonics for rhetoric, not dialectic. And it is right that discussion should have centred on this. But it would be bold to say, as L. A. Post does (in the course of making an otherwise excellent point), 'the development of an artificial system of memory is appropriate only to a teacher of rhetoric' (*loc. cit.*, p. 106.). Admittedly, Aristotle is likely to have thought memorization just as useful for the student of rhetoric as for the student of dialectic (see e.g. *Rhet.* 1396^{b}4). But since his most explicit remarks concern its use for dialectic, I shall here confine myself to this.

[2] Plato, *Protagoras* 335A.

[3] For a lively and enlightening account, see Gilbert Ryle, *Plato's Progress*, Cambridge, 1966.

[4] *Top.* 158^{a}15–17; 160^{a}17–34; *Soph. El.* 171^{b}3; 172^{a}16–17; 172^{b}16–21; 175^{b}8–14; 175^{b}28–38; 176^{a}3–18; 177^{a}20–32.

[5] *Top.* 161^{a}9–12; *Soph. El.* 183^{a}24–6.

[6] *Top.* 158^{a}10–11; 160^{b}17–22; *Soph. El.* 165^{a}15–17; 169^{b}30–2.

[7] *Top.* VIII.11.

[8] *Top.* 155^{b}26–8; 161^{a}21–4; *Soph. El.* 175^{a}31–6; 176^{a}21–3.

[9] *Top.* 100^{a}29–^{b}25; 108^{a}33–7; 112^{a}9–11; 161^{a}23–4; 161^{a}33–4; *Soph. El.* 165^{a}38–^{b}11; 171^{b}6–37.

[10] *Top.* 100^{a}29–^{b}25; *Soph. El.* 171^{b}7–11.

or by a party to the debate, or by some philosopher who is under discussion.[1]

But what is the importance of dialectical debating for Aristotle? For one thing, the two-man debating just described is close in many of its procedures to solitary thought processes. Aristotle's definition of dialectical reasoning, as reasoning that starts from premises which are *accepted* (*Top.* 100ᵃ29–ᵇ23), applies equally to two-man and to one-man processes. And he allows the name of dialectic to both. Furthermore, he expects great benefits from dialectic, either in its one-man or in its two-man form. Not only does the two-man variety sharpen the wits of would-be philosophers in various ways,[2] preparing them for one-man thought processes. But also, in one form or the other, dialectic can be used to criticize or establish very general principles of thought, such as the law of contradiction.[3] Moreover, the two-man form can be used to criticize, the one-man form to arrive at, the specialized principles of individual sciences.[4] In this last role, one-man dialectic occupies a large part of Aristotle's corpus, provided that we take the notion of dialectic in a wide enough sense. For he often reaches the first principles of a given subject by starting out from opinions 'accepted' by others.[5]

Now Aristotle is scornful of the training that his predecessors had given in dialectical debate. For they had simply handed out ready-made arguments to be memorized. Aristotle comments that they were imparting not the art of dialectical debate, but its products.[6] One might as well offer to impart skill in obviating footache, and then supply shoes instead of instruction in shoemaking. Aristotle is not opposed to his students memorizing arguments. What he objects to is the idea that their training should be confined to this. He wants his own students to memorize arguments,[7] definitions,[8]

---

[1] *Top.* 159ᵇ8–35; 161ᵇ34–162ᵃ3.

[2] *Top.* 101ᵃ34–6; 163ᵇ9–16; *Soph. El.* 175ᵃ5–12.

[3] *Metaph.* 1004ᵇ15–27; 1005ᵇ22; 1006ᵃ16–28 (the two-man variety here); 1012ᵃ17–23; *Rhet.* 1355ᵃ8–10.

[4] *Top.* 101ᵃ36–ᵇ4; *Soph. El.* 172ᵃ19.

[5] See G. E. L. Owen, 'τιθέναι τὰ φαινόμενα', in *Aristote et les Problèmes de Méthode*, Proceedings of the 2nd Symposium Aristotelicum, ed. S. Mansion, Louvain and Paris, 1961.

[6] *Soph. El.* 183ᵇ35–184ᵃ10.

[7] *Top.* 163ᵇ4–164ᵇ19.

[8] *Top.* 163ᵇ20.

the theses of various schools,[1] and most important of all *topoi*, or general patterns of argument, such as he has given in Books II to VII of the *Topics*.[2]

In the main passage where he urges his students to memorize *topoi* (*Top.* 163[b]22–33), he does not actually call the rules he is talking about *topoi*. But it is clear that this is what they are.[3]

Not only does Aristotle want his students to memorize these general patterns of argument, but also he speaks of the process of recollecting them in visual terms. The student should be able to take a mental look (*blepein* 163[b]31–2) at them classified by numbers. Evidently the memorizing and recollection are thought of as involving imagery. And this is confirmed when we note that in the immediately preceding three lines, 163[b]28–30, Aristotle explicitly compares these patterns, in respect of their utility, to the places,

---

[1] *Top.* 105[b]16–18; *Soph. El.* 172[b]31–2.

[2] *Top.* 154[a]14; 163[b]22–33, esp. 32. An example of a *topos* would be the following (*Top.* 113[a]33–5): 'If someone has postulated an accident that has a contrary, see if the subject which receives the accident could also receive its contrary. For a single subject can receive contraries.' The point of this rule is to show how one can defend or attack the postulation of the accident. For example, suppose someone has said he is certain he has two hands. You can reply (if this *topos* is correct) that if he is capable of certainty about this, he must be capable of uncertainty about it. For a single subject can receive contraries.

The *topos* is a general pattern of argument, rather than an argument, because it is supposed to apply not merely to certainty and uncertainty, but to black and white, good and evil, and any pair of contraries. There is a distinction, however, between common *topoi* (or commonplaces) and proper *topoi*. The latter are restricted in subject matter to Physics, Geometry, Ethics, or some other special field. The former are unrestricted, and so 'common' to all fields (see *Rhet.* 1358[a]2–32; *Top.* 119[a]12–24).

[3] This is the view taken by Alexander of Aphrodisias (*ad loc.*). The evidence for it is assembled by W. A. De Pater, 'La fonction du lieu et de l'instrument dans les *Topiques*', in *Aristotle on Dialectic*, Proceedings of the 3rd Symposium Aristotelicum, ed. G. E. L. Owen, Oxford, 1968. Thus Aristotle calls the rules he is here talking about 'headings under which arguments very often fall' (163[b]22–3), i.e. general patterns of argument. Cf. the definition of *topos* at *Rhet.* 1403[a]18–19, as 'a heading under which fall many rhetorical syllogisms'. Aristotle also refers to the rules in our passage as 'common' (163[b]32), i.e. as common *topoi*, rather than proper *topoi*. He calls them 'starting-points' (163[b]27–8; [b]33), and 'premises' (163[b]28; [b]32), and compares them with the 'elements' in geometry (163[b]24). This is probably because they form the point from which one starts, in attacking or defending the claim that has been made. Cf. also the equation of *topoi* with elements at *Rhet.* 1403[a]18–19. Finally, he calls the rules 'hypotheses' (163[b]33) because they are starting-points that are assumed, not proved.

i.e., to the background images of places, used in the place system of mnemonists.

The Greek word for places is '*topoi*'. And it has been plausibly suggested, for example by Solmsen,[1] on the basis of the present passage, that the otherwise rather mysterious practice of referring to the general patterns of argument as common *topoi*, or common-places, is derived from the mnemonists' talk of places.

Aristotle's application of the word '*topos*' to general patterns of argument is the source of the name of his treatise, '*The Topics*'. And this use of the word, along with the related use in rhetoric, is the source of the English expressions 'topic' and 'commonplace'. If the above suggestions are correct, these words will have come *via* Aristotle ultimately from the system of place memory. It has been suggested that the phrase 'in the first place' also comes from this system.

Aristotle was not alone in thinking that memorizing was important for students of dialectic, and in recommending that they should recollect visually, through some kind of imagery. When he complains that his predecessors had handed out ready-made arguments to be memorized, he mentions in particular Gorgias, who trained his students in rhetoric, not dialectic. He may also have in mind Protagoras, who appears to have written a book or books full of dialectical arguments,[2] and who certainly fits the description that Aristotle gives here, when he refers to people who took fees in connexion with eristic arguments (183ᵇ37). But a more tangible relic exists of the kind of training of which Aristotle complains, namely the *Dissoi Logoi*. This work is included by Diels in his *Die Fragmente der Vorsokratiker*, and he dates it to around 400 B.C.[3] It is a catalogue of arguments on both sides of various controversial issues, including the one so much debated by Plato as to whether virtue is teachable. The last section offers advice on memorizing. It is plausible to suppose that the author intended the preceding arguments to be memorized. In some of his advice, the author seems to envisage that his readers will use visual imagery, when they memorize. For example, if they wish to remember the name 'Chrysippus', they should place it on *chrusos* (gold) and *hippos*

---

[1] *Die Entwicklung der aristotelischer Logik und Rhetorik*, Berlin, 1929, pp. 170–175.

[2] Plato, *Sophist* 232D–E.

[3] English translation in *Mind* 1968, by Rosamond Kent Sprague.

(horse). Or if they want to remember the name 'Pyrilampes', they should place it on *pur* (fire) and *lampein* (to shine).

It is possible, then, that there was a tradition of interest in mnemonics in connexion with dialectical training. It should be stressed that the mnemonic techniques recommended to students at *Top.* 163ᵇ31–2, and in the last section of the *Dissoi Logoi*, are not examples of the place system. Again, there is no example of the place system in Aristotle's *De Memoria*. But all these passages describe techniques that involve some use of imagery. Moreover, there is one mnemonic technique described in the *De Memoria* which has proved difficult to understand. This is the technique of mid-points. We may find we can understand it a little better if we bring to bear on it our knowledge of the place system.

The technique of mid-points

The technique of mid-points is described in *DM* 452ᵃ17–24. Here Aristotle is giving advice on recollecting, and he recommends starting one's search from the middle of a batch of associated ideas. Though the text does not say so, it helps if we assume that the recollecting is being done through some system of images. For without a system of images, it would be hard to skip over members of the series, landing precisely in the middle of a batch. And it would also be hard to vary the direction of travel along the series. Yet most commentators assume that these operations are being recommended.[1]

A number of Greek letters appear in the text. But the manuscripts are agreed only on A B Γ Δ E Z H Θ in line 19, on Γ as second letter in line 22, and on A as last letter in line 23. Over other letters they disagree seriously. This constitutes one of the problems for the interpreter. The translation below, of course, incorporates the readings I want to argue for. At this stage of the argument, the reader should remain open-minded as to which letters should be read.

Aristotle's advice may perhaps be reconstructed as follows. A B Γ Δ E Z H Θ are images. His recommendation concerns not the middle of the whole series, but the middle of each triplet, EZH, BΓΔ, etc. Each image, or perhaps the middle image of each

---

[1] Our interpretation will assume in addition that one is being advised to visit the adjacent items on either side of a given one.

triplet, may contain a numerical symbol.[1] The images were formed originally in order to stand for certain items which we were memorizing, e.g., the points in a speech. When we wish to recollect the memorized items, we do so by scanning the images. Suppose we wish to recollect one of the items memorized, and don't know where it comes in the series. For example, suppose we thought we must report one of the points in the speech to a friend, and have forgotten what the point was. We could plod through every image in turn, in order to recollect. But Aristotle recommends skipping some images, so as to increase speed. We should go (if unsuccessful with the endmost image in the series, Θ) to the middle image in the next triplet along. From that point we can easily visit the images that are next door on either side.[2] If unsuccessful, we should then move to the middle of the next triplet along, and so on.

The rationale will be that it is easy to visit the images that are next door on either side. Consequently, if we follow the more obvious method of plodding through every image in order, we waste effort, because at each new position we will have only one unexplored next door neighbour, instead of two.

The idea that Aristotle is talking of the middle of each triplet, and not the middle of the whole series, can be supported as follows.

(i) Lines 18–19 say, 'A person will remember when he comes to this, or else he will no longer remember from any position.' This would seem an unwarranted thing to say of the middle of the whole series.

(ii) Lines 19–23 pick out not one base (the middle of the whole series) from which we can remember, but a succession of four bases. Which of these bases could be the middle of the whole series? None of the first three, for none of these provides a last chance for us to remember ('a person will remember when he comes to this, or else he will no longer remember from any position' lines 18–19). But not the fourth base either, for this, so far from being a 'starting-point' (line 17), would be a finishing-point. Moreover it would provide a last chance not in virtue of being in the 'middle' (line 17), but merely in virtue of being reached last.

---

[1] Cf. *Rhetorica ad Herennium* III.18, which recommends incorporating the image of a golden hand with five fingers within the fifth image in a series, and the image of a friend named Decimus (Tenth) within the tenth.

[2] Cf. Luria, pp. 32–3, Hunter, pp. 215–16, who say it is easy to take a look at the images next door on either side, given the vivid images used in mnemonics.

(iii) In a series of eight members there is no middle. Yet all the mss. agree on giving eight letters in line 19. And there is independent evidence that Aristotle intended eight, in that lines 20–3 mention exactly eight visiting-points.

(iv) In order to get a reference to the middle of the whole series, one is forced to read letters that are not in the mss. at a good number of places (e.g., W. D. Ross does so five times), and even at places where the mss. are agreed (e.g., W. D. Ross does so twice).

(v) It is hard to see what advantage there would be in starting from the middle of the whole series.

These difficulties are avoided, if we take the reference to be to the middle of each triplet. First, lines 18–19 make good sense. The point will be that, if the thing to be recollected is connected with one member of a triplet such as EZH, then we ought to be able to recollect it when we take as our base Z, the middle member of the triplet. Otherwise, we never will. Secondly, the interpretation is supported by the fact that Aristotle has us visit a succession of bases, and that, in connexion with each of the second and third bases, two further visiting points are mentioned. Thirdly, no difficulty arises from the fact that the mss. cite a series of eight letters which lacks a centre. Fourthly, letters not in any mss. are (for what this is worth) read only twice (Z and H at lines 20 and 21), and (more importantly) never at a point where the mss. agree. Fifthly, there is a definite point to Aristotle's suggestion, if he is speaking of the middle of each triplet, namely that it is economical to make sure you have two unexplored next door neighbours at every move, instead of one. Sixthly, his suggestion is thus made to turn on the idea that it is easy to visit next door neighbours on either side, and this fits with what modern writers say about systems of mnemonic images (Luria, pp. 32–3; Hunter, pp. 215–16).

As interpreted above, Aristotle is making some psychological assumptions, namely that it is possible (*a*) to alternate directions of travel along the series, and that it is particularly easy (*b*) to visit the next door neighbours on either side of a member. He also assumes that it is possible (*c*) to skip over members of a series, and land precisely in the middle of a batch. Is Aristotle likely to have made these assumptions?

(i) The assumption that (*a*) and (*c*) are possible is commonly attributed to Aristotle by other interpretations. So the attribution is not a peculiar difficulty for the present interpretation.

(ii) In any case, (*a*), (*b*) and (*c*) are made comparatively easy by the vividness of the images used in mnemonics.

(iii) The easiness of (*b*), or something like it, is explicitly mentioned by Luria and Hunter, as we have seen.

(iv) The possibility of doing something like (*a*), namely running through a series in either direction, is mentioned by Seneca (*Controversiarum Libri*, Lib. I, Praef. 2), by the *Rhetorica ad Herennium* (III, 17–18), by Luria (pp. 31–3), and by Hunter (p. 215).

(v) (*c*) would be more difficult. But it would be made easier by the incorporation of a symbol within the middle image of each batch of three, in the manner suggested in the *Rhetorica ad Herennium* (III, 18), or by the incorporation of a numerical symbol within every image.

3. Recollection

Etymology of anamimnêskesthai

There is an important fact about the Greek verb *anamimnêskesthai*, which I translate 'to recollect'. Grammatically speaking, it is passive in form, the passive of the verb 'to remind'.[1] So grammar suggests it should mean 'to be reminded'. It is for this reason that Plato says in the *Phaedo*[2] something which wouldn't be true of the English verb 'to recollect', nor of the English verb 'to remember'. Recollection, he says, involves one thing putting you in mind of another. Similarly, Aristotle analyses recollection as involving a succession of associated ideas.[3] To illustrate, if you think of Cebes straight off, you are not recollecting Cebes. But if you are put in mind of Cebes by seeing Cebes' friend, Simmias, this is, or may be, recollection.

In the word *anamimnêskesthai*, the prefix *ana-* means again, and the rest of the word is related to Aristotle's two standard verbs for remembering. Etymology might then suggest that recollection is the recovery of memory. But Aristotle denies this,[4] on the grounds that memory need not have preceded recollection. Rather, recollection is the recovery of scientific knowledge, perception, etc.[5]

Sources of Aristotle's interest in recollection

So much by way of introduction. We shall get clearer about what recollection is, as we go along. But now I want to ask why Aristotle should have devoted half his treatise to this apparently specialized subject. For he has devoted all the second chapter, except for the section on judging temporal distances. Two answers may be suggested. First, recollection played a major role in Plato's metaphysics and epistemology. And though Aristotle did not accept the metaphysics and epistemology, he did inherit the interest in recollection.

---

[1] It is passive rather than middle, as can be seen from the formation of the future and aorist tenses.

[2] 73C–74D. Cf. *Meno* 82E for the idea that recollection involves a succession of steps (*ephexês*—the same word is used by Aristotle, 451ᵇ18; ᵇ27; 452ᵃ2).

[3] *DM*451ᵇ10–452ᵃ7.

[4] 451ᵃ21–31. See note on 451ᵃ20–1 for other grounds that Aristotle could have given for his denial.

[5] 451ᵇ2–5.

Secondly, recollection played an important part in the training of students for dialectical debate. Let us take these answers one at a time.

Recollection is of great importance in the theory of Plato's *Meno* and *Phaedo*, because it constitutes the only route to knowledge of the standard subjects of dialectical inquiry. Examples of such subjects are the Equal, the Greater and the Less, the Beautiful, the Good, the Just and the Holy. We gain knowledge of these by a dialectical process that is accompanied by, or culminates in, recollection.[1] As to why Plato thinks recollection is the route to knowledge of such things—we shall consider this further below.[2] Recollection gains added importance in both dialogues. For if we acquire knowledge of these things by a process of recollection, this fact can be used to argue for the discarnate existence of the soul before birth. For our ability to recollect these things implies our prior knowledge of them. And the only available time in which we can have acquired such prior knowledge, it is argued, is the time before birth. Though Aristotle does not accept any of this theory, he will naturally have inherited from it a strong interest in recollection.

Plato makes a second link between dialectic and recollection. Not only does dialectic culminate in recollection, but also the conduct of a dialectical discussion requires the participants to recollect relevant data. Taking four dialogues, I note that Plato refers to the need for such recollection three times in the *Meno*,[3] twice in the *Euthydemus*,[4] once in the *Protagoras*,[5] and once in the *Theaetetus*.[6] This is something with which Aristotle would very much agree. Indeed, he takes it a stage further. He thinks the ability to recollect is so important for successful dialectical debating, that he urges his students to memorize certain things, in order to prepare themselves for such debates. And he gives similar advice to students of rhetoric (see pp. 27–31). This supplies him with a second reason for his interest in recollection.

---

[1] *Meno* 80D–86C; *Phaedo* 72E–77B. It is by a process of dialectical questioning that the slave boy in the *Meno* is led to 'recollect' mathematical truths. In the *Phaedo*, it is explicitly said that such 'recollection' is possible on all the subjects studied by dialectic, and the above list of subjects is given (75C–D).

[2] pp. 37–40.

[3] *Meno* 71C–D; 73C; 76A–B.

[4] *Euthydemus* 279C; 287B.

[5] *Protagoras* 349A–B.

[6] *Theaetetus* 166E.

How recollection differs from relearning

I want next to discuss the analogies that Plato finds between recollection and certain cases of learning, and the treatment that Aristotle gives to some of these analogies, especially when he discusses how to distinguish recollection from relearning. In his *Meno* and *Phaedo* Plato puts forward the thesis that what we call learning is recollection.[1] He shows some inclination to think it should be called recollection instead of, not as well as, learning.[2] But as he is by no means consistent about this, I shall sometimes speak of it as learning, and not always use the more cautious phrase, 'what we call learning.' He draws on at least five analogies between certain cases normally classified as learning and certain cases of recollection. Of these analogies I want to concentrate on two, because Aristotle has something to say about them.

The first analogy is this. Plato distinguishes between two kinds of learning.[3] In one, the learner simply absorbs information transmitted from a teacher. In the other, the learner works things out and sees them for himself. Dialectic is especially fitted to produce the second kind of learning. For in dialectical discussion, the answerer has to decide for himself what the right answer is to the questions that are put to him. The slave boy, allegedly, has to do this in the *Meno*, where Socrates insists four times that he is not teaching the boy.[4] And this creates the first point of analogy with recollection. For recollection is defined in three works as involving getting knowledge not from the external, but from the internal, world. In *Meno* 85D, *Phaedo* 75E, and *Philebus* 34B–C, it is said to be the recovery of knowledge which is one's own, from within oneself. Thus, it is like the second kind of learning process, in that it does not involve absorbing knowledge transmitted from someone else.

---

[1] *Meno* 81D–86B; *Phaedo* 72E; 73B; 75E–76C.

[2] 'We do not learn' (Meno's formulation at *Meno* 81E); 'what is *called* learning' (*Meno* 81D; 81E; *Phaedo* 73B; 75E; 76A). But sometimes these strictures are missing: 'our learning is recollection' (Cebes' formulation at Phaedo 72E); 'learning is recollection' (*Meno* 81D; Phaedo 76A); 'tried to seek or learn' (Meno 84C).

[3] E.g. *Republic* 518B–C. Cf. the midwife analogy of *Theaetetus* 149A–151D. A number of commentators discuss the distinction. But I am especially indebted to an unpublished paper by Professor Steven Tigner, 'The Gross Structure and Development of Plato's Theory of *Anamnesis*'. This paper also picks out three of the five analogies I shall be mentioning.

[4] *Meno* 82B; 82E; 84D; 85D.

Admittedly, some readers are incredulous at Plato's claim that the boy is working things out for himself. They complain that Socrates' questions are leading ones, and that the boy is to some considerable extent dependent on the appearance of diagrams drawn for him in the sand. I personally believe that the slave boy can be said to be seeing things for himself. But at any rate, even a sceptical reader can agree to the following. There do exist cases of learning in which the learner works things out for himself. And these will be analogous to recollection, in that the knowledge is not acquired merely from the external world.

A second analogy is this. Recollection involves an association of ideas. And learning also sometimes involves an association. Thus our learning about the Equal itself involves an association between ordinary equal things in this world and the Equal itself (*Phaedo* 74A–D). Again, when we learn by reasoning something out, we pass through a succession of associated steps. The slave boy, for example, passes through such a succession (*ephexês*, *Meno* 82E).

Now what does Aristotle have to say about these first two analogies? He criticizes the theory that what we call learning is recollection in the *Prior Analytics* (67^a8–27) and *Posterior Analytics* (71^a30–$^b8$). In the *De Memoria*, he assumes the theory false, but he does not discuss it (though some commentators think he is discussing it in 451^a21–5). The relation of recollection to learning comes up in a quite different connexion at 451^b6–10, where he discusses a special case of learning, namely learning for a second time, or relearning. He has said that recollection is the recovery of scientific knowledge, perception, etc. (451^b2–5). He realizes that this statement is not enough, however, to distinguish recollecting from relearning. So he asks how these differ. And his answer is (452^a4–12) that the man who recollects is able to move somehow through his own agency from the first idea in a series on to what follows. Neither in recollecting, nor in remembering, does one depend on someone else. Presumably, in learning, and in relearning, one does so depend.

Unfortunately, Aristotle is doubly wrong, or at least misleading, where Plato had been doubly right. First, as far as learning something, and relearning it is concerned, a man can do this through his own efforts, and without depending on someone else. Plato is drawing attention to this in the *Meno*, when he says that the slave boy, whom we describe as learning, is getting knowledge from within himself, and hence recollecting. Why does Aristotle miss this truth, that some learning, and some relearning, is achieved without dependence on someone else? One factor is perhaps this. In Greek there was a tendency—and I call it no more than a tendency—to use one of the words for discovering (e.g. *heuriskein*) for cases of acquiring knowledge through one's own unaided efforts. It was slightly less natural to use one of the words for learning (e.g. *manthanein*).[1]

As for Aristotle's claim about recollection not being dependent on others, this too leaves something to be desired. In saying that the man who recollects acts somehow through his own agency, he is faithful to Plato's point that in recollecting one recovers knowledge from within oneself (*Meno* 85D; *Philebus* 34B–C). In fact, the phrase translated 'of himself' at 452ᵃ11 is exactly the phrase used in the *Meno* (*ex hautou*). But Plato had none the less allowed a considerable amount of memory-jogging during the recollective process. This jogging might come either from Socrates' questioning (*Meno* 80D–86C), or from the perception of something associated with the thing recollected (*Phaedo* 73C–74A). Aristotle does not discuss, but veils under the word 'somehow' (*pôs* 452ᵃ5), the question of how much memory-jogging is permissible. Martin and Deutscher have argued that, in the case of the related concept of remembering, the permissible amount is very considerable.[2]

So much for the first of Plato's analogies. What about the second, that learning, like recollection, can involve an association of ideas? For when one learns by reasoning something out, one passes through a succession of associated steps in the reasoning. Aristotle underlines this second analogy, when he argues that recollection is, as it were, a sort of reasoning process (453ᵃ9–14). Moreover, when he gives examples of the kind of association of ideas involved in recollection, he cites the steps in a chain of mathematical reasoning (452ᵃ3). He may be conscious that this creates an analogy between some cases of relearning and recollection. For when he tries to distinguish these, he envisages that both the relearner and the

---

[1] For some kind of contrast between discovery and learning, see Archytas, fragment 3, in Diels, *Die Fragmente der Vorsokratiker*; Plato *Cratylus* 436A, 438A–B, 439B; *Phaedo* 85C; *Laches* 186E; Aristotle *DA* 429ᵇ9. Notice also that Plato, insofar as he uses either word, finds it more natural to say that the slave boy is discovering things (*Meno* 84B; 84C; cf. 86B–C), than to say that he is learning them (cf. 81D; 84C).

[2] *Op. cit.*, pp. 182–5.

recollector will have to pass from the first step in a series on to what follows (452ᵃ6). And he tries to locate the difference between them elsewhere, namely in the question of whether they depend on someone else's help.

Three further analogies are argued for by Plato. They are that the learning of something can be (i) preceded by, and also (ii) made possible by, earlier knowledge of that same thing (*Meno* 85D; *Phaedo* 74D–75A). Of course, if one is learning the thing afresh, one's earlier knowledge must have been temporarily lost in the interim. But so too one who recollects may have (iii) temporarily lost the knowledge he once possessed (*Meno* 85C–D; 86A–C; *Phaedo* 73E; 74B–C; *Philebus* 34B–C). We may not be convinced that Plato's cases of learning are analogous to recollection in these last three ways. But none the less Martin and Deutscher have argued that there do exist cases of learning, that is, cases of learning for a second time, which are analogous in just these ways to remembering.

It is harder, then, than Aristotle supposed to distinguish recollection from relearning. The analogies exploited by Plato help to bring out the difficulty. They provide a valuable corrective to Aristotle's attempted distinction, whatever our verdict may be on Plato's own theory that what we call learning is recollection.

Ordinary language examples of recollection

A further comparison between Plato and Aristotle will be useful. For in the *Phaedo* (73C–74A), Plato offers us some everyday examples of recollection. And from these it looks as if Aristotle goes beyond ordinary language in his account of what recollection is. It will be an everyday instance of recollection, if we are reminded of a man by seeing his cloak. In this example, there is no deliberate search for the man. Nor is the recollective process triggered by our thinking of something, but simply by our seeing it. Aristotle's account of recollection differs in both respects.

He calls recollection a search, or at least something like a search (453ᵃ12; ᵃ15; cf. ᵃ25). And he discusses no cases in which one is reminded of something without having searched for it. (Line 451ᵇ23 does not introduce such a case, but only a case in which one has not searched for a special kind of short cut.) He also says that recollection is a form of reasoning, or something like it, a process too intellectual to belong to lower animals. It belongs only to animals that can deliberate, in fact of the known animals only to man

(453ª6–14). It looks as if he thinks of it as something deliberately undertaken.[1] This, then, is one way in which he diverges from ordinary language.

Another way in which he diverges is by concentrating exclusively on cases in which recollection starts from one's thinking of something, not from one's perceiving it. The divergence here is less sharp, however, in that he says recollection starts when an appropriate 'change' (*kinêsis* 451ᵇ11) occurs within one. This word 'change' could be applied to an act of sense-perception (see 450ª31), even though he does not here so apply it.

In the Platonic examples just mentioned, the more natural translation for *anamimnêskesthai* is perhaps 'being reminded' rather than 'recollecting'. So it might be said that Aristotle's analysis is faithful for those cases where the more natural translation is 'recollecting'. Elsewhere, Aristotle himself, like Plato, uses the verb *anamimnêskesthai* of cases where there has been no deliberate search, e.g. at *NE* 1166ᵇ15, where he speaks of wicked men being reminded of unpleasant things against their wills.

How recollection differs from remembering

The above comparisons with Plato may make it a little clearer what sort of thing recollection is. But to complete our clarification, we should make three further points. A successful recollective search culminates in remembering. But recollecting is not the same thing as remembering. How do they differ? One distinguishing feature, of course, is that recollection involves an association of ideas. Aristotle refers to three further distinctions at 453ª4ff. One concerns the time of occurrence. Though memory need not precede recollection (451ª21–31), it can do so, because it can start with almost no gap, after the original perception or learning. Recollection, however, presupposes a gap, during which the perception or knowledge is lost (451ª31–ᵇ6). The second distinction concerns the different kind of bodily constitution that the two processes call for, which has the result that different people are good at recollecting and at remembering (449ᵇ6–8). The third distinction consists in the more intellectual character of recollection, which results in its being confined to man (453ª7–14).

---

[1] He comes closer to discussing examples of the *Phaedo* type in *Insom.* 460ᵇ3–16, but without calling them cases of recollection.

Search-verb or find-verb?

A possible source of confusion is that it is sometimes the search, whether successful or not (453ᵃ12; 22), sometimes the act in which a successful search culminates, or the search viewed as successful (451ᵃ6; ᵇ2–5; 452ᵃ7–8; ᵃ28–9; 453ᵃ16–18; ᵃ20), that is called recollection.

Two kinds of recollective process

A final point of clarification is this. Aristotle seems to have two kinds of case in mind. In one, we start with an image of the thing we later recollect, but fail at first to refer the image to the thing. Only after passing through a series of associated images, do we manage to refer it. A case like this seems to be envisaged at 451ᵃ5–8. In other cases, we start by passing through a series of associated images, and reach the image of the thing we recollect only at the end of this process.

Association of ideas

For someone who comes to Aristotle's account of recollection with the concerns of a modern philosopher, the most interesting aspect may well be his treatment of the association of ideas. In this, Aristotle owes a debt to Plato. For in the *Phaedo* (73D–74A) Plato had already given examples that illustrate two of Aristotle's laws of association.[1] And though he had not formulated laws, he did comment that the relation between associated items is not always one of similarity.

The first formulation of the laws of association is usually attributed to Aristotle. This is on the basis of his account in 451ᵇ19–20 of how one is reminded of a thing by something similar, opposite, or neighbouring.

Much of the interest of this idea derives from its subsequent history. Locke, Berkeley and, still more, Hume made use of the principle of association of ideas. Indeed, Hume wrote of himself, in his anonymous *Abstract*: '. . . if anything can entitle the author to so glorious a name as that of an *inventor*, it is the use he makes of the principle of the association of ideas, which enters into most of his philosophy.' The principle of association helped the empiricists to

[1] One can be reminded of Cebes by seeing Simmias, who is often close to him (neighbouring). And one can be reminded of Simmias on seeing a picture of him (similar).

explain our powers of thinking consistently with their view that our ideas are derived from experience, and that they are not innate. On the other side, Leibniz argued that the principle of association of ideas can account only for the kind of behaviour based on experience that is found as much in beasts as in men. But men are capable of genuine reasoning, which is something different from the mere association of ideas, and which requires innate ideas (*Nouveaux Essais sur l'Entendement Humain*, Avant-Propos; II.II.II; II.33; *Théodicée, Discours de la Conformité* (etc.), 65; *La Monadologie* 26–9). After the appearance of Hume's *Treatise*, Hartley in the 18th century and James Mill in the 19th, represented all operations of the mind as different modes of the association of ideas. James Mill applied his theories of association to the upbringing of his son, J. S. Mill. Hartley and James Mill were followed by many others. Aristotle's three 'laws' were often repeated, and there were discussions as to whether one or another of the 'laws' could be dropped, or one reduced to another.

Aristotle himself is more sober. When dealing with mental operations other than recollecting, he does not refer back to his discussion of the association of ideas, though he would have had opportunity to do so, e.g. in his treatment of people who mistake what is merely similar to a thing for the thing itself (*Insom.* 460^{a}32–^{b}27; 461^{b}7–462^{a}8), or of people who like a certain odour because it belongs to food which they like (*DS* 443^{b}17–445^{a}16), or of people who judge by sight that something is sweet, or judge from its yellow-ness that it is gall (*DA* 425^{a}22; ^{b}3–4), or judge that a pale thing seen is a certain person (*DA* 418^{a}20–4; 425^{a}24–7; *An. Post.* 43^{a}35–6; 83^{a}1–14). Much less is he inclined then to reduce all mental operations to modes of the association of ideas.

But if, in the analysis of mental operations, he does not exaggerate the importance of association of ideas, is it equally true that, in the analysis of association, he does not exaggerate the importance of the three relations, similar, opposite, and neighbouring? When he introduces these three relations (451^{b}19–20), he is describing a special case of recollecting. In this case, a person chooses to start in his thoughts from something similar, opposite, or neighbouring to that which he wishes to recollect. If he wants to recollect what he did last Tuesday, he starts with what he did last Monday, which is neighbouring. By this means, with any luck, he will be led straight from his starting-point to the thing he is seeking, and so he will have taken a short cut. This is by no means the usual case, however. For the most part (451ᵇ24), one has to pass through other, earlier images ('other' *heterôn* 451ᵇ24; 'earlier' *proterôn* 451ᵇ17; 'distant' *porrhô* 451ᵇ26), before one reaches an item that will lead one straight on to what one is seeking. Does this mean that it is only in special cases that associated items are linked by the relations, similar, opposite, neighbouring? No. It is only in special cases that one seeks out in advance (451ᵇ22–3; perhaps 451ᵇ27–8) a starting-point that will be similar, opposite, or neighbouring to the thing one wishes to recollect, and so takes a short cut. But Aristotle gives other examples (451ᵇ26; 452ᵃ3; 452ᵃ14–16; 452ᵇ5) in which items are associated as similar, opposite, or neighbouring. Moreover, he says that in 'most' (451ᵇ24) cases, although one passes through 'other' images before reaching the penultimate one, the images are still 'like' (*hoiôn* 451ᵇ25) those described in connexion with the short cut. And whether one passes through a long chain of images or a short one (as in the case of the short cut, and perhaps in other cases too), the method of recollecting is the same (451ᵇ27). Although the only respect of sameness explicitly mentioned is that each image is linked to its successor by habit, we are entitled to suppose that in 'most' cases, or at least in some, another respect of sameness will be that the imaged items are related to each other as similar, opposite, or neighbouring. On the other hand, nothing so far said implies that these relations are involved in all cases of recollection.

It may be thought that Aristotle must have supposed they are involved in all cases. For he says that recollection is made possible by the fact that certain images are *naturally* fitted (451ᵇ11) to follow each other. It is hard to see why they should be *naturally* fitted to follow each other, unless it be because of some relationship between the things imaged, e.g. the relationship of being similar, opposite, or neighbouring. But in spite of appearances, Aristotle does not claim that in *all* cases of recollection one image is naturally fitted to follow another. His point may simply be that unless there were *some* cases of this kind, there would not have been any cases of recollection. For although images can be made to follow each other by artifice, instead of by nature, when this happens, art is merely imitating nature.

In fact, Aristotle seems very much alive to the idea that artifice, rather than nature, may influence the order in which images occur. He mentions the artificial system of place-memory at 452ᵃ13. And he mentions the part played in memorizing by deliberate repetition

(451^a13-14). Now, one can memorize in a fixed order fifty names, or fifty numbers, selected at random, either by dint of repeating them to oneself in a certain order, or by using a method such as the place-system. The names or numbers need not be similar, opposite, or neighbouring to each other.[1] In fact, they need not have any significant relationship of their own, apart from what is given to them by the thoughts or images of the man who is memorizing. These thoughts or images have an order of their own. And by means of this, order is imposed on the things he is memorizing. It would be a considerable oversight, if Aristotle, with his interest in artificial memory systems, overlooked this fact. It is to be hoped that he did not.

The idea that similar, opposite and neighbouring are the only relations recognized will receive a further blow, if, in the list of items at 452^a14-16, air is related to whiteness by the fact that air bubbles make foam white (GA $735^a30-736^a22$; 784^b15; 786^a7-13). Such a relationship is not one of being similar, opposite, or neighbouring. In Plato's *Phaedo* too, some of the illustrations do not fit neatly under Aristotle's three 'laws'. For example, one can be reminded of Cebes by seeing a picture of his friend, Simmias ($73E$).

We have so far been speaking of the relations between things imaged, not between images. For in spite of the name 'association of *ideas*', the relations similar, opposite and neighbouring are put forward as holding between things imaged. As for the relations between images themselves, Aristotle speaks of them as following each other in a certain order 'by habit' (451^b13; $^b14$; $^b18$; $^b28$).[2] How is habit related to the other factors we have mentioned, to nature, artifice, and the relations of similar, opposite and neighbouring?

It looks as if Aristotle's view is that, whenever images regularly follow each other, this is by way of habit. The habit may have become established either because the images were naturally fitted (451^b11) to occur in a certain order, or (assuming he consciously recognizes this alternative) as a result of artifice. As for the relations of similar,

[1] Unless one stretches the sense of these words grotesquely, as some nineteenth-century thinkers did, and claims, for example, that the numbers are neighbouring to each other because one's utterances of the numerals, as one memorizes, come one after another.

[2] By 'habit' here, he means a certain kind of tendency, but not necessarily (451^b14-16) one established by dint of repetition.

opposite and neighbouring, they simply serve to create the natural tendency just mentioned.

A final complication is that the relations of similar, opposite and neighbouring can have an effect, even in the absence of habit. Such is the situation when one is trying to recollect a person's name, and blunders onto a name that is merely similar to the one sought (452^{a}30–^{b}6). In this example, it is similarity that has caused the wrong name to be associated in a group with the right one. But the move is not a matter of habit. For the order of images is not due to habit, unless it is a regularly occurring order; whereas the present move is unwonted and exceptional. So it is not a matter of habit, but may even be contrary to habit.

De Memoria et Reminiscentia

Translated, with interpretative summaries

CHAPTER ONE

Programme

449ᵇ4 In discussing memory and remembering, it is necessary to say what they are, and how their occurrence is to be explained, and to which part of the soul this affection, and recollecting, belong. For it is not the same people who are good at remembering and at recollecting. Rather, for the most part, slow people are better at remembering, while those who are quick and learn well are better at recollecting.

First main topic. The object of memory. This is the past, not the future or present, nor what is present as an object of perception or theorizing. But after perception or theorizing is over, one can remember, and in doing so, will remember the fact of having perceived or theorized.

449ᵃ9 First, then, one must consider what sort of things the objects of memory are, for this often leads people astray. For it is not possible to remember the future, which is instead an object of judgment and prediction. (There might even be a predictive science, as some people say divination is.) Nor is memory of the present; rather, perception is, for by perception we know neither the future nor the past, but only the present. But memory is of the past. No one would say he was remembering what was present, when it was present, e.g. this white thing when he was seeing it; nor would he say he was remembering the object of his theorizing when he was in the act of theorizing and thinking. Rather he says simply that he is perceiving the one, and exercizing scientific knowledge of the other. But

47

when a person possesses scientific knowledge and perception without actually exercizing them, under these conditions he remembers in the one case that he learned or theorized, in the other that he heard, or saw, or something of the kind. For whenever someone is actively engaged in remembering, he always says in his soul in this way that he heard, or perceived, or thought this before.

Conclusions. Memory is not identical with, but subsequent to, perception and conception. It is a state or affection connected with these. Only those animals which can perceive the time-lapse can remember.

449ᵇ24 Therefore memory is not perception or conception, but a state or affection connected with one of these, when time has elapsed. There is no memory of the present at the present, as has been said. But perception is of the present, prediction of the future, and memory of the past. And this is why all memory involves time. So only animals which perceive time remember, and they do so by means of that with which they perceive.

Second main topic. To what part of the soul does memory belong? Two reasons why it belongs to the perceptual part. (a) It involves cognizing time. Time must be cognized in the same way as magnitude and change, since these are three interrelated continua. We know, then, from our discussion of cognizing magnitude that the cognition will be by means of images. (b) Memory also involves cognizing the thing remembered. And this too is done by means of images. Any connexion between memory and the intellect is merely incidental.

449ᵇ30 An account has already been given of imagination in the discussion of the soul, and it is not possible to think without an image. For the same effect occurs in thinking as in drawing a diagram. For in the latter case, though we do not make any use of the fact that the size of the triangle is determinate, we none the less draw it with a determinate size. And similarly someone who is thinking, even if he is not thinking of something with a size, places something with a size before his eyes, but thinks of it not as having a size. If its nature is that of things which have a size, but not a determinate one, he places before his eyes something with a determinate size, but thinks of it simply as having size. Now the reason why it is not possible to think of anything without continuity, nor of things not in time without time, is another story. But it is necessary that magnitude and change should be known by the same means as time. And an image is an affection belonging to the common sense. So it is apparent that knowledge of these is due to the primary perceptive part. Memory, even the memory of objects of thought, is not without an image. So memory will belong to thought in virtue of an incidental association, but in its own right to the primary perceptive part.

Corollaries. But for this, memory would not belong to animals lower than man, and perhaps to no mortal animals. Even as it is, it does not belong to those animals which lack perception of time.

450ᵃ15 And this is why some other animals too have memory, and not only men and those animals that have judgment or intelligence. But if memory were one of the thinking parts, not many of the other animals would have it, and perhaps no mortal animals would, since even as it is, they do not all have memory, because they do not all have perception of time. For, as we said before, when someone is actively engaged in memory, he perceives in addition that he saw this, or heard it, or learned it earlier; and earlier and later are in time.

Summary
450ᵃ22 It is apparent, then, to which part of the soul memory belongs, namely the same part as that to which imagination belongs. And it is the objects of imagination that are remembered in their own right, whereas things that are not grasped without imagination are remembered in virtue of an incidental association.

Third main topic. An impasse. Why it arises. Memory involves an image in the soul, which is among other things a sort of imprint in the body of a former sense-image. (A suitable surface is needed in the body to take the quasi-imprint.)

450ª25 One might be puzzled how, when the affection is present but the thing is absent, what is not present is ever remembered. For it is clear that one must think of the affection, which is produced by means of perception in the soul and in that part of the body which contains the soul, as being like a sort of picture, the having of which we say is memory. For the change that occurs marks in a sort of imprint, as it were, of the sense-image, as people do who seal things with signet rings.

450ª32 (And this is also why memory does not occur in those who are subject to a lot of movement, because of some trouble or because of their time of life, just as if the change and the seal were falling on running water. In others, because of wearing down, as in the old parts of buildings, and because of the hardness of what receives the affection, the imprint is not produced. And this is why the very young and the old have poor memory, since they are in a state of flux, the former because they are growing, the latter because they are wasting away. Similarly the very quick and the very slow are also obviously neither of them good at remembering. For the former are too fluid, the latter too hard. Therefore with the former the image does not remain in the soul, while with the latter it does not take hold.)

The impasse. What it is. How by contemplating and perceiving this image does one remember something quite distinct from it?

450ᵇ11 But then, if this is the sort of thing that happens with memory, does one remember this affection, or the thing from which it was produced? For if the former, we would remember nothing absent; but if the latter, how is it that while perceiving the affection we remember the absent thing which we are not perceiving? And if it is like an imprint or drawing in us, why should the perception of this be the memory of a different thing, rather than of the affection itself? For one who is exercizing his memory contemplates this affection and perceives this. How therefore will he remember what is not present? For at that rate one could also see and hear what is not present.

Solution. One contemplates the image as being of, i.e. as being a copy of, something distinct.

450ᵇ20 Or is there a way in which this is possible and happens? For the figure drawn on a panel is both a figure and a copy, and while being one and the same, it is both, even though the being of the two is not the same. And one can contemplate it both as a figure and as a copy. In the same way one must also conceive the image in us to be something in its own right and to be of another thing. In so far, then, as it is something in its own right, it is an object of contemplation or an image. But in so far as it is of another thing, it is a sort of copy and a reminder. So again when the change connected with the other thing is active, if the soul perceives the image as something in its own right, it appears to come to one as a thought or image. But if one contemplates the image as being of another thing, and (just as in the case of the drawing) as a copy, and as of Coriscus, when one hasn't seen Coriscus, then (not only in the case of the drawing is the experience of so contemplating it different from when one contemplates it as a drawn figure; but also) in the case of the soul, the one image occurs simply as a thought, the other, because it is a copy (as in the case of the drawing), is a reminder.

Corollaries of this solution. The possibility of regarding, or not regarding, one's image as a copy helps to explain four phenomena. (a) Doubt as to whether one has memory. (b) Suddenly switching to remembering. (c) Wrongly supposing one has memory. (d) Memorizing.

451ᵃ2 And for this reason, when changes like this are produced in our soul as a result of former perception, we sometimes do not know whether this is happening in accordance with the previous perception, and are in doubt whether it is memory or not.

451ᵃ5 At other times it happens that we have a thought and recollect that we heard or saw something earlier. This happens when one changes from contemplating the image as the thing that it is to contemplating it as being of something else.

451ᵃ8 The contrary also happens, as it did to Antipheron of Oreus and other mad people. For they used to speak of their images as things that had occurred and as if they were remembering them. This happens whenever someone contemplates what is not a copy as if it were.

451ᵃ12 Exercizes safeguard memory by reminding one. And this is nothing other than contemplating something frequently as a copy and not as a thing in its own right.

Retrospect

451ᵃ14 Now, it has been said what memory and remembering are, namely the having of an image regarded as a copy of that of which it is an image, and to which part in us memory belongs, namely the primary perceptive part and that with which we perceive time.

CHAPTER TWO

First main topic. What recollection is not. Recollection is not the recovery of memory, for no memory need have preceded. Admittedly, recollection may be the recovery of scientific knowledge, perception, etc., and so perception or the acquisition of scientific knowledge must have preceded. But it does not follow that memory must have preceded, for perception and the acquisition of scientific knowledge do not presuppose prior memory, nor incorporate within themselves the acquisition of memory, nor are they immediately followed by remembering.

Recollection is not the acquisition of memory. For remembering, followed by memory, can precede any act of recollection.

Recollection cannot even be defined simply as the recovery of scientific knowledge, perception, etc., if we want to distinguish it from relearning.

451ᵃ18 It remains to speak about recollecting. First, then, one must take as being the case all that is true in the essays. For recollection is neither the recovery nor the acquisition of memory. For when someone first learns or experiences something, he does not recover any memory, since none has preceded. Nor does he acquire memory from the start, for once the state or affection has been produced within a person, then there is memory. So memory is not produced within someone at the same time that the experience is being produced within him. Further, at the indivisible and final instant when the experience has first been produced within, although the affection and scientific knowledge are already present in the person who had the experience (if one should call the state or affection scientific knowledge—and nothing prevents us also remembering in virtue of an incidental association some of the objects of our scientific knowledge), none the less remembering itself, does not occur until time has elapsed. For a person remembers now what he saw or experienced earlier. He does not now remember what he experienced now.

451ᵃ31 Further, it is apparent that a person can remember from the start, once he has perceived or experienced something, without having just now recollected it. But when he recovers previously held scientific knowledge, or perception, or that of which we were earlier saying that the state connected with it is memory, this is, and is the time of, recollecting one of the things mentioned. (When one does remember, it results that memory follows.)

451ᵇ6 Nor indeed do these things in all circumstances yield recollection when they are reinstated in a man who had them before. Rather, in some circumstances they do, in others they do not. For the same man can learn and discover the same thing twice. So recollecting must differ from these cases, and it must be that people recollect when a principle is within them over and above the principle by which they learn.

Second main topic. Prerequisites and method of recollection. Prerequisites: images are naturally fitted to occur in a certain order, and will do so, if not of necessity, then by habit.

451^{b}10 Acts of recollection happen because one change is of a nature to occur after another. If the changes follow each other of necessity, clearly a person who undergoes the earlier change will always undergo the later one. But if they follow each other not of necessity but by habit, then for the most part a person will undergo the later one. It can happen that by undergoing certain changes once a person is more habituated than he is by undergoing other changes many times. And this is why after seeing some things once, we remember better than we do after seeing other things many times.

Method: sometimes one takes a short cut, and chooses a starting-point which (because it is similar, opposite, or neighbouring) will lead one straight to the thing one wishes to recollect. The image corresponding to such a starting-point comes next to, or overlaps with, or is the same as, the image of the thing to be recollected. But for the most part, one has to pass through other images first, before one reaches the image of the penultimate item in the series. Even so, the method of recollecting is the same as when one takes a short cut, if one considers how each item in the series is related to its successor.

451^{b}16 Whenever we recollect, then, we undergo one of the earlier changes, until we undergo the one after which the change in question habitually occurs.

451^{b}18 And this is exactly why we hunt for the successor, starting in our thoughts from the present or from something else, and from something similar, or opposite, or neighbouring. By this means recollection occurs. For the changes connected with these things in some cases are the same, in others are together, and in others include a part, so that the remainder which one underwent after that part is small.

451ᵇ22 Sometimes, then, people search in this way. But also when they do not search in this way they recollect, whenever the change in question occurs after another one. And for the most part it is after the occurrence of other changes like those we spoke of that the change in question occurs. There is no need to consider how we remember what is distant, but only what is neighbouring, for clearly the method is the same. (I mean the successor, not having searched in advance, and not having recollected.) For the changes follow each other by habit, one after another.

Method (cont.). The importance of getting a starting-point.

451ᵇ29 And thus whenever someone wishes to recollect, he will do the following. He will seek to get a starting-point for a change after which will be the change in question. And this is why recollections occur quickest and best from a starting-point. For as the things are related to each other in succession, so also are the changes. And whatever has some order, as things in mathematics do, is easily remembered. Other things are remembered badly and with difficulty.

Recollecting and relearning distinguished in light of the above. He who recollects can move on to what follows the starting-point without the help of someone else.

452ᵃ4 And recollecting differs from relearning in that a person will be able somehow to move on by himself to what follows the starting-point. When he cannot, but depends on someone else, he no longer remembers. Often a person is unable to recollect, at a given moment, but when he searches he can, and he finds what is sought. This occurs when he excites many changes, until he excites a change of a sort on which the thing will follow. For remembering is the presence within of the power which excites the changes, and this in such a way that the man moves of himself and because of changes that he possesses, as has been said.

The importance of starting-points (resumed).

452ª12 But one should get a starting-point. And this is why people are thought sometimes to recollect starting from places. The reason is that people go quickly from one thing to another, e.g. from milk to white, from white to air, and from this to fluid, from which one remembers autumn, the season one is seeking.

The middle member of a triplet makes a good starting-point. If unsuccessful with the first triplet, one should skip on to the middle member of the next triplet.

452ª17 In general in every case the middle also looks like a starting-point. For if no sooner, a person will remember when he comes to this, or else he will no longer remember from any position, as for example if someone were to think of the things denoted by A B Γ Δ E Z H Θ. For if he has not remembered at Θ, he will remember at Z for from here he can move in either direction to H or to E. But if he was not seeking one of these, after going to Γ he will remember, if he is searching for Δ or B, or if he is not, he will remember after going to A. And so in all cases.

The possibility just mentioned of moving to alternative destinations from the same starting-point explains why from a given starting-point one sometimes remembers and sometimes does not. Habit may divert one to the wrong destination. Alternatively, so may similarity. The method of recollecting has now been described.

452ª24 The reason why one sometimes remembers and sometimes does not, starting from the same position, is that it is possible to move to more than one point from the same starting-point, e.g. from Γ to Z or Δ. So if a man is moved through something old, he moves instead to something to which he is more habituated. For habit is already like nature. (And this is why what we think of frequently we recollect quickly. For just as by nature one thing is after another, so also in the activity. And frequency creates nature.)

452ª30 But just as among natural events there occur also ones contrary to nature and the result of luck, still more is this so among events that are due to habit, seeing that nature does not belong to these in the same way. So a person is sometimes moved to one place and at other times differently, especially when something draws him away elsewhere from the one place. For this reason also when we have to remember a name, if we know a similar one, we blunder onto that.

Recollecting, then, happens in this way.

Third main topic. Estimating time-lapses. Remembering involves estimating time-lapses. Different time-lapses, like different spatial magnitudes, are represented by differing small scale models in one's thought.

452ᵇ7 But the main thing is that one must know the time, either in units of measurement or indeterminately. Assume there is something with which a person distinguishes more and less time. Probably it is in the same way as he distinguishes magnitudes. For a person thinks of things large and distant not through stretching out his thought there, as some people say one stretches sight (for even if the things do not exist, he can think of them in the same way), but by means of a change which is in proportion. For there are in the thought similar shapes and changes. How, then, when someone is thinking of larger things, will the fact that he is thinking of them differ from the fact of thinking of smaller things? For everything within is smaller and in proportion to what is without.

452ᵇ15 Perhaps just as one can receive in oneself something distinct but in proportion to the forms, so also in the case of the distances. It is then, as though, if a person undergoes the change

AB, BE, he constructs ΓΔ. For the changes ΑΓ and ΓΔ are in proportion. Why, then, does he construct ΓΔ rather than ZH? Is it that as ΑΓ is to AB, so is Θ to I? So one undergoes these latter changes simultaneously. But if someone wishes to think of ZH, he thinks in the same way of BE, but instead of the changes Θ, I, he thinks of the changes K, Λ. For these latter are related as is ZA to BA.

Estimating time-lapses (cont.). The image of the thing remembered and the image representing the time-lapse must occur together. One must not wrongly suppose one's image is of a certain thing. One need not know the time-lapse in standard units of measurement.

452ᵇ23 Whenever, then, the change connected with the thing and that connected with the time occur together, then one is exercizing memory. But if a person thinks he is doing this, when he is not, then he thinks he is remembering. For nothing prevents him from being deceived and thinking he is remembering when he is not. However, when exercizing his memory a person cannot think he is not doing so and fail to notice that he is remembering. For this turned out to be what remembering was. But if the change connected with the thing occurs without that connected with the time, or the latter without the former, one does not remember.

452ᵇ29 The change connected with the time is of two sorts. For sometimes a person does not remember the time in units of measurement, e.g. that he did something or other the day before yesterday; but sometimes also he does remember the time this way. None the less, he remembers, even if it be not in units of measurement. And people are in the habit of saying that they remember but don't know when, whenever they do not know the amount of time in units of measurement.

Fourth main topic. Recollecting and remembering. Differences between the two. Recollecting is too like reasoning to belong to animals lower than man.

453ᵃ4 Now, it has been said in what precedes that it is not the same people who are good at remembering and at recollecting. Recollecting differs from remembering not only in respect of the time, but in that many other animals share in remembering, while of the known animals one may say that none other than man shares in recollecting. The explanation is that recollecting is, as it were, a sort of reasoning. For in recollecting, a man reasons that he formerly saw, or heard, or had some such experience, and recollecting is, as it were, a sort of search. And this kind of search is an attribute only of those animals which also have the deliberating part. For indeed deliberation is a sort of reasoning.

Fifth main topic. Recollection involves the body. Evidence of its physiological character: some people become upset when they fail to recollect, and succeed in recollecting after giving up, which needs to be explained by saying that they have set up motion in an organ, and, once set up, the motion will not stop, until what is sought returns.

453ᵃ14 The following is a sign that the affection is something to do with the body, and that recollection is a search in something bodily for an image. It upsets some people when they are unable to recollect in spite of applying their thought hard, and when they are no longer trying, they recollect none the less. This happens most to melancholic people. For images move them most. The reason for recollecting not being under their control is that just as it is no longer in people's power to stop something when they throw it, so also he who is recollecting and hunting moves a bodily thing in which the affection resides. The people who get upset most are those who happen to have fluid around the perceptive region. For once moved, the fluid is not easily stopped until what is sought returns and the movement takes a straight course.

That a motion, once set up, may be hard to stop explains various other phenomena.

453ᵃ26 And this is also why, when cases of anger and of fear

59

set something moving, they are not halted, even though the people set up counter-movements in turn, but rather the anger and fear make counter-movements in the original direction. And the affection is like names and tunes and sayings, when one such has come to be very much on someone's lips. For after the people have stopped, and without their wishing such a thing, it comes to them to sing it or say it again.

Further evidence of the physiological character of recollection. Defects in memory can be traced to physiological conditions.

453ᵃ31 Those also whose upper parts are especially large and those who are dwarf-like have poorer memories than their opposites because they have a great weight resting on the perceptive part, and neither from the start are the changes able to persist within such people and avoid being dispersed, nor during recollecting does the movement easily take a straight course. The extremely young and the very old have poor memory because of the movement in them. For the one group is wasting away, the other growing rapidly. Further, children at any rate are also dwarf-like until late in their youth.

Retrospect

453ᵇ7 Now, it has been stated what is the nature of memory and remembering, and what it is in the soul that animals remember with, and what recollecting is, and in what manner it occurs, and through what causes.

Note on the Translation

In the preface, I have claimed to be aiming at a faithful translation. But everyone believes in faithfulness, just as everyone believes in virtue. The question is: what does faithfulness require? Sometimes this is genuinely hard to answer. For example, the phrase which I have translated 'says in his soul', at 449^b22–3, was a perfectly natural one in Greek. It could then be argued that the faithful translator will give a correspondingly natural English phrase, such as 'says to himself'. But I have had in mind the needs of the philosophical reader, who will be interested in Aristotle's use of the concept of soul. And so for his benefit I have given the less natural rendering.

On other occasions, the degree of faithfulness required will depend on the intended readership. Small liberties, designed to achieve literary elegance, or to provide additional explanation, may be quite legitimate for some purposes. But they can mislead the Greekless philosopher about the whole character of an argument, or of a philosophical view.

There are at least two special difficulties for the translator of Aristotle. The first is his use of technical terms which he has defined in other works. The care with which he gives these definitions, and the comparative consistency with which he uses the terms are a boon to the philosophical reader. But the terms pose a problem to the translator. I have tried to avoid two extremes. One extreme is to use a familiar and everyday English expression, translating *epistêmê*, for example, as 'knowledge', without giving any warning that it is a very special kind of knowledge. (I have called it scientific knowledge.) The opposite extreme is to decline to translate these technical terms into English, but simply to transliterate them (as *epistêmê*, for example), or to latinize them (as *scientia, sensus communis, per accidens*). I have tried to give renderings that are more informative than this.

A second difficulty for the translator is that Aristotle's work has not been polished for the reading public. It is a set of lecture notes, not indeed mere jottings, for it has been carefully reworked; but it represents lecture notes, all the same. This comes out in Aristotle's confusing use of the word *pathos* with different references in neighbouring lines (see notes on 450^{b}1; 451^{a}23–4). It emerges in the sentence at 450^{b}29–451^{a}2, where Aristotle sets out to discuss the case of referring a mental picture to its original, but interrupts himself three times to mention the case of physical pictures, and once to mention the case of viewing a mental picture without referring it. The reference of Aristotle's pronoun 'this', and of his conjunction 'for', is often hard to detect. Students of Aristotle must spend a good part of their time tracing the reference of 'for', but there always is a reference. Finally, Aristotle's wording is often elliptical in the extreme. (Bad examples occur at 450^{a}9–14 and 452^{a}28–30.) In cases where Aristotle's meaning is not seriously in doubt, but the Greek is perplexing, I have sometimes helped the English reader out. But I have not wanted to diverge too far from the Greek. I have benefited greatly from comments on the translation by Colin Haycraft and by an unnamed referee, and I take this opportunity of thanking them.

Notes to
De Memoria et Reminiscentia

CHAPTER ONE

The full title is *De Memoria et Reminiscentia*. In most places, I have shortened this to *De Memoria*. *Reminiscentia* is the Latin for recollection to which Aristotle devotes most of chapter two, and which, as explained on pp. 35–41, is distinct from memory and remembering.

The *De Memoria* is the second in a group of treatises known as the *Parva Naturalia*. Attempts have been made to date this group, or parts of it, either as later, or as earlier, than the *De Anima*, or part of it. Such attempts turn on alleged incompatibilities of doctrine, or on the alleged elaboration of a doctrine. But I know of no cogent reason for deciding on a relative date of composition for the *De Memoria*. Whatever the dates at which the treatises of the *Parva Naturalia* were first drafted, in their present form they are presented so as to read as a continuation of the *De Anima*. The *De Anima*'s account of sense-perception is completed first by the *De Sensu*'s account of the functions, organs, and objects of the senses, and then in the *De Memoria* and *De Insomniis* by an account of memory and dreaming, which are classed as perceptual powers. The continuous character of the exposition has been brought out by Charles Kahn ('Sensation and Consciousness in Aristotle's Psychology', *Archiv für Geschichte der Philosophie*, 1966). And the continuity is not a superficial matter of cross-references that could have been added by a later editor. As Kahn shows, if the account of the central sense-faculty is elaborated only in the *Parva Naturalia*, this is for reasons of exposition, and does not show a difference of date. Moreover, the *De Anima* is united with the first two treatises of the *Parva Naturalia*, in holding that memory, and other mental affections, are attributes both of the body and of the soul (*DA* 403ª3–25; *DS* 436ª6–10; *DM* 450ª28–9). Admittedly, this does not meet W. D. Ross's view that the second book of the *De Anima* expounds a doctrine incompatible with this one, so that this part at least of the *De Anima* has a different (and later) date. But Ross has not convincingly shown that there really is any incompatibility.

For further comment, see notes on 450ᵃ10–11; 450ᵃ28–9; 450ᵃ31–2. And for attempts at dating, see: F. Nuyens, *L'Évolution de la Psychologie d'Aristote*, translated from the Dutch of 1939, Louvain and Paris, 1948; W. D. Ross, *Aristotle, Parva Naturalia*, text, introduction, commentary, Oxford, 1955; W. D. Ross, *Aristotle, De Anima*, text, introduction, commentary, Oxford, 1961; W. D. Ross, in *Aristotle and Plato in the Mid-Fourth Century*, 1st Symposium Aristotelicum, ed. I. Düring and G. E. L. Owen, Göteborg, 1960; I. Block, 'The Order of Aristotle's Psychological Writings', *American Journal of Philology*, 1961. H. J. Drossaart Lulofs, *Aristotelis De Insomniis et De Divinatione per Somnum*, Leiden, 1947. Further references are given by D. A. Rees, in his review of Nuyens, in *Mind* 1951.

449ᵇ4 'Memory and remembering' (*mnêmê* and *mnêmoneuein*). This combination occurs at 449ᵇ3–4; 451ᵃ14–15; 451ᵇ5; 453ᵇ8–9. Probably the first is the ability or tendency (on which see pp. 1–2) as opposed to the act.

449ᵇ4–5 'What they are'—discussed throughout. 'To which part of the soul this affection belong[s]'—discussed 449ᵇ28–450ᵃ25. 'How their occurrence is to be explained'—discussed 450ᵃ25–451ᵃ14.

449ᵇ6 'For.' i.e. 'remembering and recollecting are different, for . . .'

449ᵇ7–8 'Slow people are better at remembering, while those who are quick and learn well are better at recollecting.' The rationale is as follows. Slow people contain hard surfaces (450ᵇ7–10). The hardness accounts for their being slow to receive the quasi-imprint (450ᵃ31), and hence slow to learn. But it also accounts for their being good at retaining the quasi-imprint, once it has taken, and so being good at remembering. (So Plato, *Theaetetus* 194E). Quick people are more fluid (450ᵇ7–10). The fluidity accounts for their being good at recollection, because he who recollects has to set up motion in an organ (453ᵃ22), and for this a fluid surface is needed. The fluidity also accounts for their being quick to receive a quasi-imprint, and hence quick to learn.

The fluidity may make these people quick in a second way too, i.e. not only quick to learn, but also quick to move from one image to the next (see *Div.* 464^{b}1 for quick motion of this kind, and note on 453^{a}19 for fluidity, both treated as characteristics of melancholics).

Note the *a priori* character of the reasoning on a scientific question. For modern research on the subject, see e.g. I. M. L. Hunter, *Memory*, Harmondsworth, pp. 137–40.

Three problems arise. (i) Since successful recollection culminates in remembering, how can one who is good at recollecting fail to be good at remembering? (ii) The fluidity of quick people impedes their retention of an imprint (450^{b}7–11). Yet such retention is needed if they are to recollect. So how can they be good at recollecting (449^{b}8)? (iii) Mnemonic systems will be useful only for a short period, if those who are best at using them soon lose their quasi-imprints, because of fluidity.

Solution. (i) The tendency of the quasi-imprints to be disrupted through fluidity makes a man fail to be *naturally* retentive. In this sense, he is not good at remembering. (ii) *Repetition*, however (451^{a}12–14; ^{b}13; 452^{a}26–30), can check the disruption of the quasi-imprints, and thus *by artifice* supply the retentiveness which is needed for recollection. (iii) Repetition also enables a man to recollect after a long period.

449^{b}9 'First.' Here begins the first of the chapter's three main divisions. The procedure of analysing an activity by first stating what its objects are is that recommended in *DA* 415^{a}20–2; 418^{a}7–8. A conclusion as to what memory is, and which animals have it, is drawn in 449^{b}24–9, on the basis of the discussion of objects. For the idea that perception is of the present, prediction of the future, and memory of the past, cf. Plato, *Philebus* 39D–E.

449^{b}9–10 'This often leads people astray.' i.e. mistakes about the object of an activity often lead to mistakes about the activity itself. The reference is presumably not merely to mistakes about the object of memory, but to mistakes about the object of whatever activity one is analysing, e.g. about the object of seeing, or hearing, as well as of remembering.

Professor Owen has suggested to me there may be a reference to a mistaken view in Plato, *Theaetetus* 166B, where Plato makes

Socrates offer in defence of Protagoras the view that what one remembers is different from what one previously perceives. It is a memory-image, i.e. something present, not past. I take it, however, that this could be only one mistake among others that Aristotle has in mind, in view of his remark that people are '*often*' led astray.

449^{b}13-15 'Nor is memory of the present; rather, perception is.' The present which one perceives can be a period, and not a mere instant. It is only because one can perceive periods, as well as instants, that (*DA* 425^{a}16; *Phys.* 219^{a}3-4) motion, change and the passage of time can be objects of perception. For the perception of these, Aristotle does not explicitly appeal, like William James and Bertrand Russell, to a specious present, i.e. to a whole period that is before the mind at a single instant. He may be relying on the simpler idea that at a given instant one perceives that same instant, while over a given period one perceives that same period. The closest he comes to the idea of a specious present is perhaps in 451^{a}29-31 (see note), where he speaks as if, at any given instant, the present has a certain span, and includes within itself experiences which one has just had.

449^{b}15 'But memory is of the past.' Not, however, of the immediate past, according to 451^{a}29-31. There the immediate past seems to be treated as part of the present. For comment on the claim that memory is of the past, see pp. 13-14.

449^{b}15-18 'No one would say.' In English, one can say of something one is seeing that one remembers it, meaning that one recognizes it. But in Greek it is more natural to stick to the word for recognizing, *anagnōrizein*. (Compare Russell, who claims that recognizing differs from remembering, *The Analysis of Mind*, pp. 168-70.) This is why no one, in Aristotle's opinion, would say he remembered a thing while he was seeing it. He would say instead that he recognized it.

Aristotle would be wrong if he denied that one could remember a thing, in the sense of having a certain ability or tendency, at the time one was seeing it. Certainly, Plato speaks in *Theaetetus* 191D and 192D as if in this *dispositional* sense one remembers a man at the time of seeing him. So we should assume Aristotle is talking of the *act* of remembering. (See note on 449^{b}22 for further confirmation.) But why would no one say that he remembered a thing at the time of theorizing about it? Perhaps Aristotle's idea is that a person who is exercising scientific knowledge (*epistasthai*, 449^{b}18) of a proposition, and theorizing about it (*theôrein*, 449^{b}17), is not merely contemplating the proposition itself, but also contemplating the reasons for it, and deducing the proposition from premises that state the reasons. This is what scientific knowledge (*epistêmê*) involves according to the *Posterior Analytics*. One who is doing all this, will not say that he is remembering the proposition. For the process is one of *working out* something and is therefore not one of remembering it.

449^{b}15 'When it is present.' i.e. when it is present to the senses, or (judging from Aristotle's second example in line 17) when it is present (at least in certain ways) to the mind. But this involves a different sense of 'present' from the temporal sense that we had earlier. So the point is not relevant for establishing that one doesn't remember the (temporal) present. What is present in one sense need not be present in the other. (Not even that which is present to the senses has to exist in the present, if we may take the example of seeing defunct stars, an example unavailable to Aristotle.) To take the examples he actually gives of things present to the mind or senses, the object of scientific knowledge would, on some views, be a timeless truth. But Aristotle would count it (*Phys.* 222^{a}5) as existing at all times, i.e. throughout the past, present, and future. And the white thing mentioned in 449^{b}17 is also likely to exist in the past, present, and future.

The point made here, though irrelevant to the earlier claim that one can't remember the present, is relevant to the later claim that memory is not identical with, but subsequent to, perception and conception.

It would be a serious mistake if Aristotle maintained quite generally that one cannot remember what is present to consciousness. For this would rule out all remembering.

449^{b}17 'Theorizing' (*theôrein*). At 450^{b}18–451^{a}13, this word and its cognates have the sense of 'contemplate'. But here Aristotle has in mind a more specialized idea. *Theôrein* now refers, first, to the actual exercize of knowledge, in contradistinction to its mere possession (cf. 'possesses . . . actually exercizing' 449^{b}19). It refers, secondly, to a special kind of knowledge, the scientific knowledge (*epistasthai*) with which it is connected in the next line. (Compare the use of the adjective *theôrêtikê*, 'theoretical', which marks off the three *scientific* branches of knowledge, mathematics, philosophy of nature and theology, from the 'practical' and 'productive' branches, *Metaph.* 1025ᵇ25–1026ᵃ23). In exercizing scientific knowledge, according to Aristotle, a man *works out* a conclusion, and derives it syllogistically from premises. It is because he is *working out* his conclusion that he would not naturally describe himself as *remembering* it.

449ᵇ20–21 'That he learned.' Lines 449ᵇ15–18 led us to expect we should be told under what conditions one can remember *the thing learnt*. But here instead Aristotle tells us under what conditions one can remember *the fact of having learned it*. Why the switch? Probably he means that under the conditions specified one remembers the thing learnt, but this inevitably involves (449ᵇ22–3) remembering the fact of having learned it. And he concentrates on the latter because it is the basis for his conclusion (449ᵇ28–9) that memory belongs only to those animals that can appreciate the time lapse since the original learning. 'For' in 449ᵇ22, will be justifying the switch to remembering the fact of having learned.

In 449ᵇ20, the mss. read 'that the angles of a triangle are equal to two right angles'. If this is retained, we should construe: 'He remembers, with regard to the fact that the angles of a triangle are equal to two right angles, in the one case that he learned it, or theorized about it, in the other case that he heard, or saw it, or something of the kind.' But this involves rather a strain on the Greek. And also we should have expected to be given in addition to this example, which is a typical object of thought, a second one that would be a more typical object of perception. It is probably better, therefore, to choose one of the recognized alternatives, of deleting the words, or transferring them to 449ᵇ17, where they would provide an example of something that is being theoretically contemplated.

The usual construction of the mss. reading is more objectionable still ('he remembers that the angles of a triangle are equal to two right angles, in the one case because he learned it or theorized about it, in the other case because . . .'). Not only does the 'because' clause seem irrelevant, but also if Aristotle had written this, he would have been likely to realize some of the difficulties for his view that one remembers the past, and not what is present. For the equality to two right angles is not merely past, but, according to the doctrine of *Phys.* 222^{a}5, omnitemporal. Moreover, such things are acknowledged (449^{b}15–18) to be present, i.e. present to the mind, at the time of being made objects of theorizing, and would surely be present to the mind equally at the time of being remembered.

449^{b}22 'Actively engaged in remembering.' Further evidence that Aristotle is discussing the act of remembering, not the ability or tendency, in these lines.

449^{b}22–3 'He always says in his soul that he heard . . .' For comment, see pp. 9–10.

449^{b}24 'Therefore.' Aristotle is now able to conclude that memory is not identical with, but subsequent to, perception and conception, and that it belongs only to those animals that can appreciate the time lapse since the original perception or conception.

449^{b}24 'Conception' (*hupolêpsis*). The term covers three species of intellectual activity, namely scientific knowledge, judgment, and intelligence (*epistêmê, doxa, phronêsis, DA* 427^{b}25). It is here contrasted with perception (*aesthêsis*). There is a similar contrast between perception and one or more forms of intellectual activity above in 449^{b}15–23, and below in 449^{b}30–450^{a}25.

449^{b}25 'State or affection' (*hexis* or *pathos*). For the phrase, see also 451^{a}23–4; ^{a}27–8. The affection turns out to be an imprinted image. The state is the ability to stir up this image (see note on 452^{a}10). A *pathos*, in its broadest sense, is anything one undergoes (*paschei*). A *hexis* is here a state, though elsewhere it is sometimes the having of something. (This corresponds to two meanings of the verb *echein*. For the translation 'having', see note on 451^{a}15–16.) Aristotle says that *pathê* of the soul are accompanied by pleasure or pain, and affect our judgment, we are said to undergo change (*kineisthai*) when we have them, they are not the result of deliberate choice, and they are comparatively short-lived and easily removed (*NE* 1105^{b}19–28; 1106^{a}3; ^{a}5; 1157^{b}28–31; *EE* 1220^{b}13–14; *Rhet.* 1378^{a}20; *Cat.* 8^{b}26–9^{a}13; 9^{b}33–10^{a}10). An example of such a *pathos* would be anger, or in the present context a memory-image. A *hexis* of the soul, he says, is something of longer duration, in accordance with which we are well or ill disposed in relation to *pathê*, for example, are good tempered (*NE* 1105^{b}19–28; cf. *Metaph.* 1022^{b}10–12).

In the present instance, the *hexis* of memory is something in accordance with which we are well disposed in relation to memory-images.

Pathos is normally translated 'affection', but for the rendering 'experience', see note on 451ᵃ23-4, for the rendering 'effect', see 450ᵃ1, and for the rendering 'trouble', see note on 450ᵇ1.

449ᵇ25 'When time has elapsed.' It is added in 451ᵃ25–31 that not only is the state or affection subsequent to the original act of learning or experiencing something, but even after the state or affection has been engendered, a further time-lapse is required before a man can remember.

449ᵇ28 'So.' This claim would follow from the one in 449ᵇ22–3 about what one says in one's soul. And it is connected with this in 450ᵃ19. But it does not follow from the more recent claims that memory is connected with a past perception or conception, and that its object is past.

449ᵇ29 'Perceive time.' For the phrase, see 450ᵃ9–12; ᵃ19; 451ᵃ17. To perceive the passage of time while it is passing is different from remembering a time-lapse. It is the latter that is mentioned at 452ᵇ30, and one would think it was the latter that was involved in remembering that one perceived or conceived something previously. Why, then, does Aristotle talk of perceiving, rather than of remembering, time? Perhaps he is anxious to emphasize that remembering a time-lapse is a perceptual, not an intellectual, activity. For this is essential for his theory that remembering is a function of the perceptual faculty, not of thought.

449ᵇ30 'That with which they perceive' (cf. 451ᵃ17; 453ᵇ9). This phrase is better than 'the perceptive part' (and the similar expressions used at 450ᵃ11; ᵃ14; ᵃ17; 451ᵃ17; 453ᵃ13; ᵃ24; ᵇ2), because it makes clear that it is the animals which do the perceiving. Strictly speaking, the part of the soul or body does not do the perceiving, as Aristotle points out when he is being more careful (*DA* 408ᵇ13). In another respect, the two phrases are on the same footing. For they do not on their own make it clear whether the reference is to a part of the soul (as it is here, and at 450ᵃ11; ᵃ14; ᵃ16; 451ᵃ17; 453ᵃ13), or whether it is to a part of the body (as at 453ᵃ24; ᵇ2). This ambiguity makes it easier for Aristotle to slide between talking about parts of the soul and parts of the body. I have avoided the translation 'faculty', because it would conceal this important ambiguity in the Greek phrase, and because it would wrongly encourage the attribution to Aristotle of the kind of 'faculty' psychology that belongs to later periods.

449^{b}30 to 450^{a}25 constitutes the second main division of the chapter. It discusses which part of the soul memory should be assigned to, and, starting at 450^{a}15, it draws corollaries concerning which animals can have memory.

Aristotle contrasts thought (*nous*) with perception (*to aisthêtikon*). He decides that memory is connected with perception, and that any connexion with thought (or intellect) is merely incidental. I have used the translation 'thought' rather than 'intellect' at 450^{a}13, in order to preserve consistency of rendering throughout the passage. But the translation 'intellect' here would have brought out one aspect of the argument. For the word *nous* is used at this point in quite a narrow sense. Thus, nothing lowlier than judgment and intelligence (*doxa* and *phronêsis* 450^{a}16) here counts as *nous*. Earlier in the passage, Aristotle's use of cognate words is wider than this. It covers thinking of one's image as having size, or not as having size.

Even when we notice how narrow a sense the word has at 450^{a}13, we may still be surprised at Aristotle's decision that memory is only incidentally connected with *nous*. For surely he ought to allow that all remembering involves judgment (*doxa*). It is supposed, after all, to involve 'saying' (*legein*) in one's soul that one encountered the imaged thing before (449^{b}22–3), and 'thinking of' (*noein*) or 'knowing' (*gnôrizein*) the time elapsed (452^{b}7–453^{a}4), not to mention regarding one's image as a copy (450^{b}20–451^{a}16).

On the other hand, Aristotle sees that if he connects memory up too closely with judgment, he will not be able to ascribe it to the lower animals, as he wants to (450^{a}15–16). Perhaps he should have concluded there was something wrong with his requirement that one should say in one's soul one encountered the imaged thing before (a requirement that gets him into other difficulties as well—see pp. 9–10).

It looks (see second note on 450^{a}13–14) as if he reaches his conclusion by confining his attention to a rather limited question. He asks whether the things we remember are *all* objects of thought, and whether they are *defined* as such, or whether many are not rather objects of perception. Alternatively, he may be asking whether our ability to remember is ever *due to* the fact that the thing remembered

F

and the time-lapse cognized are objects of thought, rather than due to the fact that they are imageable. Since his answer is 'no', he thinks he can conclude that memory's connexion with thought is only incidental. But surely there might be other reasons for saying that memory is connected in its own right with thought. One reason would be the supposed fact that memory involves 'saying' in one's soul one encountered the imaged thing before. Another reason would be the supposed fact that memory involves 'thinking of' and 'knowing' the time elapsed.

He may hope to avoid these difficulties by claiming that at 450ᵃ13 he switches to using the word *nous* in a yet narrower sense than we have supposed. Elsewhere, he allows that time-lapses are, in some sense, objects of thought (449ᵇ30–450ᵃ12; 452ᵇ7–453ᵃ4). But at 450ᵃ13 the word *nous* is reserved for a more limited range of intellectual activities. It is even misleading to say that *nous* turns out at 450ᵃ16 to include judgment (*doxa*). For by 'judgment' at 450ᵃ16, he means something very restricted, namely judgment based on reasoning (cf. *DA* 434ᵃ11, and see note on 450ᵃ16). The gist of this interpretation, then, is that Aristotle protects his claim that memory's connexion with *nous* is only incidental, by using the word *nous* in a very restricted sense. Correspondingly, just as the notion of *nous* is contracted, so the notion of perception is expanded. Thus awareness of a previous encounter, and of the lapse of time, is sometimes classed as the work of perception (see notes on 449ᵇ29; 450ᵃ19–21), not of *nous*. Indeed, that time-lapses are cognized by the perceptual faculty is explicitly argued at 450ᵃ9–12. But it is hard to see why *nous* is not also involved, until we notice the contraction in the notion of *nous*.

449ᵇ30 Imagination (*phantasia*) was discussed in *DA*, III, 3, just before the discussion of thinking, and also in 432ᵃ9–14; 433ᵃ9–12; ᵃ27; ᵇ28–30; 433ᵇ31–434ᵃ10. The kind of imagination that concerns Aristotle here is the power of having images (*phantasmata*, a cognate word). For it is this that is involved in thinking. There are other kinds of imagination, but at one point Aristotle brings up in an if-clause the idea that in the literal sense *phantasia* is just this power, the power of having images (*DA* 428ᵃ1–2).

Exercizing *phantasia* is not the same as making a judgment, according to Aristotle, and does not even involve it. This is important because it means that animals can have *phantasia*, the necessary condition of memory, even if they lack judgment (*doxa* 450ª16), and in general the power of thought (*nous* 450ª13).

449ᵇ31–450ª1 'It is not possible to think without an image.' So also *DA* 431ª16; 431ᵇ2; 432ª3–14. Contrast Plato, *Republic* 510B, 511C, 532A. Reasons why Aristotle may have held this view are offered on pp. 5–7. A related view is that the intelligible forms which are the objects of thought reside in the images (431ᵇ2; cf. 432ª3–6). Also related is the theory that to acquire a universal concept is to acquire a certain kind of image (*An. Post.*, II, 19). The relevance of the present lines depends on how we construe 450ª9–14. See note on 450ª9–14, stages (ii) and (viii), for one interpretation of the relevance.

The *De Memoria* is an important source for Aristotle's theory of thinking. It supplements the official account of *De Anima*, III, 4–8. In thinking of, say, triangles, we form a mental picture of a triangle, and attend to some features of our picture, while neglecting others. In thinking of certain spatial magnitudes, we form a small-scale picture of the magnitudes, and use the picture as a small-scale model. It is possible to see from these accounts why thinking is supposed to involve images that are like the thing thought of (see pp. 6–7), in what sense the triangle, or other object of thought, is thought of 'within' an image (*DA* 431ᵇ2), and in what sense the triangle may be said to be abstracted (e.g. *DA* 403ᵇ15; 429ᵇ18; 431ᵇ12; 432ª5).

450ª2 'Do not make any use.' Compare Berkeley, *A Treatise Concerning the Principles of Human Knowledge,* Introduction xvi.

450ª2–3 Size (*to poson*) has two species, the continuous (mentioned 450ª8) and the discrete (*Cat.*, ch. 6). Examples of what is continuous are spatial magnitude (*megethos*), change and time (mentioned 450ª9–10). An example of what is discrete is a numerable aggregate, e.g. a quartet of musicians.

450ª5 'Places . . . before his eyes.' This process, involved in all thinking, was compared at *DA* 427ᵇ18 to the activity of summoning up mnemonic 'places'.

450ª7–9 'It is not possible to think of anything without continuity.' Since one can evidently think of things that lack size (450ª4), one must be able to think of things which lack continuity, and presumably to think of them as lacking continuity. (Confirmed *DA* 429ᵇ10–22.) What one cannot do, as we have just learnt, is to think of them without the aid of an image. And an image has size, even though the object of thought may be sizeless (449ᵇ30–450ᵃ7). Indeed, the image has spatial continuity, and, as the next phrase may imply, it can also have temporal continuity.

'Nor of things not in time without time.' The sense of 'not in time' is explained in *Phys.* 221ᵃ7–ᵇ5. It involves not being shorter in duration than, and hence encompassed by, time. Examples of things not in time: the heavenly bodies (221ᵇ3–5), the incommensurability of diagonal and side (222ᵃ5).

1. One can't think of things not in time without the aid of an image (or other thought-process) that takes time. Admittedly, some thinking does not take time, but only if the object of thought is simple (*DA* 430ᵇ15; *Metaph.* 1016ᵇ1). Now the incommensurability of diagonal and side is complex, since it involves a combination of ideas. And the heavenly bodies are complex, in that they consist of matter and form. So at least some of the things that are not in time can't be thought of without the aid of a time-lapse for thinking.

2. Alternatively, the sense may be that one can't think of things not in time as altogether divorced from time. For the incommensurability of diagonal and side, though not in time, must be thought of as existing always (*Phys.* 222ᵃ5). Similarly, the heavenly bodies move, and their movement has duration.

450ᵃ9–14   I propose the following interpretation.

I. (i) Magnitude, change and time, being three interrelated continua (see the *Physics*), must be cognized by some one thing.

(ii) But we have seen (450ᵃ1–7) that magnitude is cognized by means of an image. (Not expressed.)

(iii) Now an image is an affection of the common sense, and of the primary perceptive part, which either is, or includes, the common sense.

(iv) So magnitude, change and time (= 'these' 450ᵃ12) are all cognized by means of the primary perceptive part.

(v) Hence, insofar as it involves cognition of time, memory is connected with the primary perceptive part. (Not expressed.)

II. (vi) Now memory involves cognition not only of time, but also of the thing remembered. (Not expressed.)

(vii) This also involves an image.

(viii) No exception is provided by memory of thinkables since (see 449^{b}30–450^{a}9) thought itself involves an image.

(ix) So on this ground too memory is connected with the primary perceptive part.

(x) Any connexion with thought is merely incidental. (Asserted on independent grounds.)

No interpretation of these lines is likely to be entirely free of difficulty. But the present one is put forward as having two advantages. First, it does not require us to transpose or expunge the sentence, 'And an image is an affection belonging to the common sense'. Secondly, it surmounts the difficulty that on many interpretations it is not clear why we need lines 450^{a}9–12 as well as 450^{a}12–14. Often, no relevance is supplied for the statements that magnitude, change and time must be cognized by some one thing (450^{a}9–10), and that the cognition of them is by the primary perceptive part (450^{a}11–12). But the present interpretation makes full use of both sets of lines. It regards them as providing two separate arguments (steps (i)–(v), and (vi)–(x)) for the same conclusion.

450^{a}10–11 'The common sense.' Not to be confused with our notion of plain common sense (although there may be an indirect relation between these). The phrase (*koinê aesthêsis*) is used only three times in Aristotle, at *PA* 686^{a}27, *DA* 425^{a}27, and here. In the second passage its role is that of apprehending the common sense-objects, i.e. those that can be perceived by more than one sense, such as magnitude or change. In the third passage its role is to apprehend images.

There is controversy over the relation between the power of perceiving the common sense-objects and a variety of other perceptual powers. Some of these other powers are connected by Aristotle with the central sense-organ, which is in the heart. And some require the existence of a kind of unity among the various powers of perception. For one view on the controversy see D. W. Hamlyn, 'Koine Aesthesis', *Monist*, April 1968. The other perceptual powers in question are those of (i) perceiving simultaneously different sense-objects (*DA* 426^{b}12–427^{a}14; 431^{a}20–431^{b}1; *DS* 449^{a}8–20), (ii) perceiving that they differ (first two of preceding references, and *Som.* 455^{a}17–18), (iii) perceiving that they belong to one thing (*DA* 425^{b}1–3), (iv) perceiving sweet by sight (*DA* 425^{a}21–4; ^{a}30–^{b}4), (v) simultaneously losing or regaining the various perceptual powers on going to sleep or awakening (*Som.* 455^{a}25–6), (vi) perceiving that we see, hear, etc. (*Som.* 455^{a}12–20), (vii) cognizing time (*DM* 450^{a}9–10), (viii) remembering (*DM* 450^{a}14; 451^{a}16–17).

On one view, the common sense is responsible for all these functions. On another view, it is responsible only for the perception of the common sense-objects, such as magnitude and change, and for the cognition of images, and hence in turn for certain activities that require imagery, such as cognizing time and remembering. The other functions, however, are assigned to something different, namely to something which is variously described as 'that which can perceive all things' (*to aisthêtikon pantôn DS* 449^{a}17–18), as 'the ability that accompanies all the senses in common' (*koinê dunamis akolouthousa pasais Som.* 455^{a}16), and perhaps as 'the primary perceptive part' (*to prôton aisthêtikon DM* 450^{a}10–11; 451^{a}17). According to a third view, doctrines concerning the common sense were elaborated by Aristotle's successors, and interpolated into Aristotle's text at various places, the only genuinely Aristotelian use of the phrase 'common sense' being at *DA* 425^{a}27, where it has no technical meaning such as Aristotle's successors gave it.

In the note on 450^{a}9–14, I assume that the 'primary perceptive part' (450^{a}11–12) either is identical with, or includes, the common sense.

I. Block takes the more elaborate account of these sense-functions which we find in the *Parva Naturalia* to be a sign that the *Parva Naturalia* was composed later than the *De Anima* ('The Order of Aristotle's Psychological Writings', *American Journal of Philology*, 1961). But Charles Kahn has convincingly argued that the greater elaboration to be found in the *Parva Naturalia* is due to reasons of exposition ('Sensation and Consciousness in Aristotle's Psychology', *Archiv für Geschichte der Philosophie*, 1966).

450^{a}11–12 'The primary perceptive part' (for the phrase, cf. 450^{a}14; 451^{a}17, and see notes on 449^{b}30 'that with which they perceive' and 450^{a}10–11 'the common sense'). Where I have written 'part', no noun is supplied in the Greek. I have chosen a noun which is ambiguous, as the Greek phrase is, between something in the body and something in the soul, though here Aristotle intends to refer to the soul.

450ª12–13 'Objects of thought.' i.e. as opposed to objects of perception. Examples were discussed in 450ª4–7.

450ª13–14 Aristotle's final statement has two halves. From the connexion, just established, between memory and images, he may be entitled to conclude that memory is connected in its own right with perception. But we must not allow him to conclude also that its connexion with thought is only incidental. (This would be a very bad argument, for thought itself involves imagery.) The claim that memory's connexion with thought is only incidental needs to be based on other grounds, not made explicit in what precedes. We can see what sort of grounds he would give, by seeing what is meant by the claim that the connexion with thought is only incidental. For this, see next note.

450ª13–14 'In virtue of an incidental association . . . in its own right' (*kata sumbebêkos* and *kath' hauto*). One's ability to remember is never *due to* the fact that the thing remembered and the time-lapse cognized are objects of thought. It is due to their being imageable. And so it is due to the perceptual faculty, not to thought. (For further clarification, see note on 450ª23–5.)

Alternatively, the meaning of *kata sumbebêkos* and *kath' hauto* may be closer to that at *An. Post.* 73ª34–b5, and *Metaph.* 1026b27–1027ª28. In that case, the point will be that the things we remember are *all* imaged, and are *defined* as being imaged, and hence are cognized with the aid of the perceptual faculty. But they are not all, nor even for the most part, objects of thought. Nor are they defined as being objects of thought. Many are objects of perception instead.

On either interpretation, Aristotle has to admit that the time-lapse cognized is, in some sense, an object of thought. This admission could prove embarrassing for his claim that memory's connexion with thought is only incidental. To combat it, he will have to switch to speaking of thought in a much narrower sense. (See note on 449b30–450ª25 for discussion of this and related embarrassments.)

450ª16 'Animals that have judgment or intelligence.' *Doxa* or *phronêsis*, two of the three species of conception (*hupolêpsis*, 449b24, and *DA* 427b25). The present passage regards them as two species of the power of thought (*nous*). Aristotle often grants intelligence (*phronêsis*) to some animals other than man. His most generous statement is in *Metaph*. 980^{b}22, where he says some have intelligence, some are also capable of learning (*manthanein*), and some even have a small amount of experiential knowledge (*empeiria*), though Alexander of Aphrodisias thinks 'small' is an understatement and means none. Judgment (*doxa*), on the other hand, appears to be denied to sub-human animals at *DA* 428^{a}19–24. Later on, 434^{a}11, on one interpretation, implies that it is only one type of judgment they cannot have, viz. that based on reasoning.

If lower animals have memory, they presumably say in their souls that they encountered the imaged thing before (449^{b}22–3), and cognize the time elapsed (452^{b}7–453^{a}4). If so, what does Aristotle mean when he implies here that judgment is not required for memory? Perhaps he means to be speaking only of judgment based on reasoning.

450^{a}16–17 'Parts' (*moria*). The word 'part' is explicit here and at 449^{b}5; 451^{a}16. That he means parts of the *soul* is clear from 449^{b}5; 450^{a}22; 451^{a}16; 453^{b}9. The parts of the soul are powers, such as the power to think, or the power to perceive. By calling these powers *parts* of the soul, Aristotle suggests that the soul *is* an (interrelated) set of powers. The phrase 'thinking parts' misleadingly suggests that a part of the soul, i.e. a power, is itself capable of thinking (cf. 450^{a}11; ^{a}14; 451^{a}17; 453^{a}13; ^{a}24; ^{b}2, for references to bodily or psychic parts that can perceive or deliberate). His more considered view is that the *man* does the thinking, in virtue of the power or part of his soul (*DA* 408^{b}13). The parts of the soul are not spatially separated, nor can a higher part exist separately from a lower part (if we ignore the active intellect); the parts differ only in their definition (see e.g. *DA* 413^{b}13–22).

450^{a}18 'Perhaps to no mortal animals.' 'Perhaps', because it depends on the kind of thinking to which the present false hypothesis assigns remembering. If remembering is assigned to the kind of thinking in which God engages, and which involves no imagery, then no mortal animals, not even man, would have memory. If remembering is assigned to the kind of thinking in which man, but not the lower animals, engage, then no animals *other* than man would have memory. If remembering is assigned to a more lowly kind of thought, e.g. to intelligence, which at 450^{a}15–16 is classed under the power of thought, then it will belong to a few of the lower animals.

The talk of mortal animals implies a reference to Aristotle's doctrine that God is an immortal animal (*Top.* 128^{b}19; 132^{b}10; *Metaph.* 1023^{b}32; 1072^{b}28; 1088^{a}10).

There is no suggestion that *as things are* God has memory, nor that *as things are* God has a part of the soul which men lack, but only that on the false hypothesis He *might* have.

The rendering 'perhaps to no mortal animals' is admittedly not without difficulty. For one thing, the reference to the imageless kind of thinking in which God indulges, but men do not, is unexpected. Many commentators prefer to emend the text and remove the word, 'mortal' (*thnêtôn*). But if we do this, we should not follow W. D. Ross, and accept Förster's emendation, 'none of the unthinking animals' (*anoêtôn*). For this would render unintelligible the hesitation implied by 'perhaps'.

450^{a}18 'Since' applies to everything from 'it would not belong' in line 17. The idea is that 'even as it is' not all animals have memory; if it were a thinking part, even fewer would have it.

450^{a}19 'For.' i.e. 'This debars them from having memory, for . . .'

450^{a}19-21 'As we said before . . . he perceives in addition that he saw this.' What Aristotle said before (449^{b}22-3) is what I have written (*proteron prosaisthanetai*), and not what is read in most mss. (*prosaisthanetai hoti proteron*). One ms. reads *proteron proaisthanetai*. For comment on Aristotle's claim, see pp. 9-10.

Aristotle is careful here to say that one perceives, rather than that one judges, or thinks, one saw such-and-such. This is necessary for his theory that memory can belong to animals incapable of judgment, and that memory is a function of the perceptual faculty, not of thought.

450^{a}23-5 The things that are not grasped without imagination are objects of thought (449^{b}31-450^{a}1). They are thought of within images (*DA* 431^{b}2). For example, in order to think of triangles, one forms a mental picture of a triangle and attends to some aspects of the picture, while neglecting others. If an object of thought can be remembered, this is thanks to the imagery within which we think of it, and not thanks to its characteristics quâ object of thought. Thus it is remembered not in its own right (*kath' hauto*), but in virtue of an incidental association (*kata sumbebêkos*).

If this is the meaning of *kath' hauto* and *kata sumbebêkos*, the meaning here is close to that at e.g. *DS* 445ᵇ28; *Cat.* 5ᵃ39 (see also *DA* 418ᵃ29–31). The idea is that an object of thought can be remembered, but only thanks to something which is different from it, namely an image.

Alternatively (see note on 450ᵃ13–14), the meaning may be that, whereas the objects of memory are all imaged, and are defined as being imaged, they are not all, nor even for the most part, objects of thought. Nor are they defined as being objects of thought. Many are objects of perception instead.

450ᵃ25 'One might be puzzled.' The rest of the chapter, apart from the summary at the end, is devoted to an impasse. 450ᵃ25–ᵇ11 tells why it arises. 450ᵇ11–20 says what it is. 450ᵇ20–451ᵃ2 solves it. 450ᵃ2–14 draws four corollaries from the solution. The discussion of the impasse forms the third main division of the chapter. The impasse (as to how awareness of the 'affection', i.e. the image, that is present can yield memory of the 'thing', which is absent) could have been suggested to Aristotle by reflection on the theory of Plato, *Theaetetus* 166ᴮ. According to this theory, what one remembers is the memory image, i.e. something present, not absent.

450ᵃ27 'For it is clear.' i.e. 'The puzzle arises because it is clear ...' On why it seems clear to Aristotle, see pp. 6–7.

450ᵃ28–9 'By means of perception.' The account of memory given here, as involving an imprint derived from perception, can apply to memory of objects of thought, just as much as to memory of things perceived. For the objects of thought reside within the imprints. (See *DA* 431ᵇ2; 432ᵃ3–6; according to which they reside in the sensible forms which the sense-organs receive during perception, and in the images that are retained after perception.) The account in Plato's *Theaetetus* also allows for remembering objects of thought, but in a different way, since it speaks of thoughts as well as perceptions being imprinted on the block of wax within us (191ᴅ). In the remainder of the present chapter, Aristotle tends to concentrate on the memory of things perceived, presumably because this is the simpler case, and because objects of thought are remembered only in virtue of an incidental association (450ᵃ24–5).

'Part of the body which contains the soul.' The heart (e.g. *Iuv.* 469ᵃ5–12. Cf. Plato, *Theaetetus* 194ᴄ–ᴇ). The location of the soul within a part of the body was taken by F. Nuyens (*L'Évolution de la Psychologie d'Aristote*, tr. Louvain, 1948) to be a feature of the middle period of Aristotle's career, though he did not in fact assign the *De Memoria* to the middle period. However, Nuyens' view that the location of the soul is a feature of the middle period has been convincingly attacked. (See I. Block, 'The Order of Aristotle's Psychological Writings', *American Journal of Philology*, 1961; W. F. R. Hardie, 'Aristotle's Treatment of the Relation between the Soul and the Body', *Philosophical Quarterly*, 1964; C. Kahn, 'Sensation and Consciousness in Aristotle's Psychology', *Archiv für Geschichte der Philosophie*, 1966.)

W. D. Ross treats the phrase 'part of the body which contains the soul' as expressing a view of the soul incompatible with, and earlier than, that in *DA* II, where the soul is called the entelechy of the body (*Aristotle, Parva Naturalia*, text, introduction and commentary, Oxford, 1955, p. 16; *Aristotle, De Anima*, edited with introduction and commentary, Oxford, 1961, p. 10). The phrase, he maintains, treats body and soul as two substances. This is by no means clear, however.

'The affection that is produced by means of perception in the soul and in that part of the body which contains the soul.' Aristotle is not talking of two effects, an image in the soul and a physical change in the body, but of one effect, namely the image. The image is in the soul (450^b10-11), but also in the body (453^a15-16). It is in the body not only because it is in the soul and the soul is in the body, and not only because it is causally dependent on a certain part of the body, but also because of the theory of *DA*, $403^a25-{}^b9$ that every mental occurrence, including an image, is, among other things, a physiological entity. This theory is sometimes summarized in a phrase that is reminiscent of the present one, by saying that mental occurrences are common to the soul and the body (*DA* 403^a3-25; *DS* 436^a6-10). The *De Sensu* passage explicitly cites memory as an example. On the physical and mental aspects of the memory-image, see pp. 14–17.

450^a29 and 31   'Like a sort of picture . . . a sort of imprint as it were.' If we are right in translating 'a sort of', rather than simply 'a', Aristotle's hesitation is considerable.

450^a30 'Having': *hexis*. See note on 451^a15-16.

450ᵃ31 'The change.' i.e. the perceptual process.

450ᵃ31 'Imprint': *tupos*.

450ᵃ31–2 'Sense-image' (*aisthêma*). The word that corresponds most closely to 'sense-datum'. Evidence as to the nature of *aisthêmata*.

(i) They are not acts of perception, but (*Insom.* 460ᵇ3) objects of perception. See also (iii) and (v).

(ii) They are not external things or qualities. For they can linger on when these have gone (*Insom.* 460ᵇ2–3). Again, it is on account of the *aisthêma* that one judges the external thing to be, say, Coriscus (*Insom.* 461ᵇ25), so that the *aisthêma* is evidently not itself the external thing.

(iii) Rather *aisthêmata* are images. For they are said to be like *phantasmata*, except in the respect that they occur in the presence of the external thing (*DA* 432ᵃ9–10). Elsewhere it is allowed that they may linger for a little while after the external thing has gone (*Insom.* 460ᵇ2–3).

(iv) Memory-images and dream-images are not *aisthêmata* (in spite of *Som.* 456ᵃ26), but rather are *phantasmata* produced by earlier *aisthêmata* (*DM* 450ᵃ30–ᵇ11; *Insom.* 462ᵃ27–31). As *aisthêmata* give rise to *phantasmata*, so in Hume's theory impressions are followed by and, as he sometimes says, are causes of ideas (*Treatise* I.I.I).

(v) *Aisthêmata* are somewhat like pictures, judging from the fact that the imprint of the *aisthêma* is like a picture (*DM* 450ᵃ27–32).

The *aisthêma* (sense-image) is never mentioned by name in Aristotle's main accounts of sense-perception, that is in the accounts of the *De Anima* and *De Sensu*. The only explicit mention to be found in these works is in connexion with the theory of thinking, where it is said that images (*phantasmata*) play the same role in thinking as sense-images (*aisthêmata*) play in perceiving. *Aisthêmata* are more frequently mentioned in the *De Memoria* and *De Insomniis*. Here again the context of the discussion is not sense-perception. Rather it is memory and dreaming. The images of memory and dreams are said to be produced by earlier *aisthêmata*. Images play a major role in the analysis of thought, memory and dreams. And it is for this reason that in these contexts we find mention of sense-images, which serve as the analogues, or as the causes, of thought-images, memory-images and dream-images.

None the less, we should not draw from these facts any conclusions about the date of composition of various writings, nor
suggest that Aristotle reached the idea of a sense-image only after
reflecting on cases where it is more plausible to postulate an image,
i.e. on the cases of thought, memory and dreams. Against this is the
fact that when he does talk of sense-images, he treats them as
something familiar, which needs no introduction. And indeed, his
discussion of sense-perception does pave the way for talking about
them. For it both discusses the coloration of the eye-jelly, which
serves as the 'material cause' or 'matter' of the visual sense-image,
and also introduces the idea of actually functioning colour (DA
425^{b}26–426^{a}26), which seems to have much in common with the
notion of a visual sensation. If he mentions sense-images by name
chiefly in his discussion of thought, memory and dreams, this is
because he has more occasion to mention them there, not because
he first thinks of them there.

450^{b}1 'Movement because of some trouble.' The tissues in the
body which are to receive the imprint are in a state of movement
because of some trouble. Aristotle confusingly uses the word *pathos*
first to refer to the imprinted image (450^{a}26; ^{a}30; ^{b}5), and then to
mean some trouble. For the implication of harm sometimes present
in the word *pathos*, see *Metaph.* 1022^{b}19.

450^{b}2–3 'The change.' i.e. the perceptual process, which was
called a change at 450^{a}31.

450^{b}3 'Wearing down.' Does this imply an unstable surface? If
so, why is it connected in the next phrase with the idea of a hard
surface? And why the implied contrast with the group mentioned
just before, who have unstable surfaces because of their age?
G. R. T. Ross (*ad loc.*) ingeniously suggests that the removal by
wear of a soft layer of plaster exposes hard stone beneath. But perhaps, more simply, the idea is of something worn smooth and hard.

450^{b}10 'With the former the image does not remain.' The former
are very quick people. But Aristotle would presumably hold the
same view about the very young and the old. 'Image': *phantasma*.

450^{b}11 'It does not take hold'—in the very slow. Even in the
moderately slow, it will not take hold easily. But when it does, it is
firmly retained. So moderately slow people do have good memory

in *one* sense, namely that they are retentive. There is therefore no contradiction with 449ᵇ7–8.

450ᵇ13 'Or the thing from which it was produced.' Evidently Aristotle does not have symbolic images in mind here. If one's image was produced by a hat, one remembers the hat, not something which the hat symbolizes. See pp. 3–4.

450ᵇ21–2 'Both a figure and a copy' (*zôon* and *eikôn*). We should reject the alternative rendering, 'For the animal drawn on a panel is both an animal and a copy'. This latter assumes that the distinction is between the animal-in-the-picture (which may be ten feet tall, and stalking its prey) and the copy (which may be two inches from top to bottom, and which cannot be said to be stalking its prey). One reason why this cannot be the distinction intended is that in the case of mental images, we are not offered a choice between regarding our image as a copy of Coriscus, and regarding it as an imaged Coriscus. If Aristotle had said this, he would have failed in his whole purpose, which is to show how our attention may, or may not, be directed to Coriscus, when we have an image of him. It is only when we regard our image as a copy, that our attention is directed to Coriscus. If the analogy is to hold between mental images and pictures, it will be only when we regard a picture as a copy that our attention is directed to the object depicted. When we regard a picture in the other way, then, our attention will not be directed to the animal-in-the-picture. We shall think of the picture simply as a figure.

450ᵇ22–3 'The being of the two is not the same.' i.e. if one were to say what a picture *is* and what a copy *is*, or what it is for a picture to *exist* and what it is for a copy to *exist*, one would not give the same account for pictures and for copies.

450ᵇ27 'Reminder': *mnêmoneuma*.

450ᵇ27 'Again' marks the transition from discussing the dual status of the mental image, to discussing the dual status of our perception of the mental image.

450ᵇ27 'The change connected with the other thing' (*hê kinêsis autou*). i.e. the image of the thing. For the image described as a change, see e.g. 451ᵃ3; 452ᵇ23. For a similar use of the distinction between change and thing, see 451ᵇ20–1; 452ᵃ1–2; 452ᵇ23.

450^{b}29–451^{a}2 'But if one contemplates it . . . is a reminder.' The passage sets out to discuss the mental image. But it is complicated by three references (which I have put in parenthesis) to the picture, at 'just as in the case of the drawing', at 'not only in the case of the drawing is the experience of so contemplating it different from when one contemplates it as a drawn picture', and at 'as in the case of the drawing'.

For comment on the requirement that one should regard one's image as being *of* something, and as being a copy of something, see p. 10.

450^{b}30–1 'When one hasn't seen Coriscus.' i.e. when one hasn't sighted him, or when one doesn't have him in sight. If one had him in sight, one would not be remembering, but only recognizing (449^{b}15–16; cf. *Insom.* 461^{b}25).

450^{b}31 'Coriscus.' A real person, a member of Aristotle's class. See W. Jaeger, *Aristotle, Fundamentals of His Development*, tr. Oxford, second edition, 1948, chapter 5; I. Düring, *Aristotle in the Ancient Biographical Tradition*, Göteborg, 1957, p. 371; H. Jackson, 'Aristotle's Lecture-Room and Lectures', *Journal of Philology*, 1920, pp. 191–200.

450^{b}31 'In the case of the drawing' (second occurrence). The Greek ambiguously says 'in this case'. The contrast is probably with 'in the case of the soul' (451^{a}1).

451^{a}2 'For this reason.' One reason is that there is a possibility of regarding, or not regarding, an image as a copy of something else. This explains (*a*) 451^{a}2–5, the possibility of doubt as to whether one should regard one's image as a copy; (*b*) 451^{a}5–8, the possibility of suddenly switching to regarding it as a copy; (*c*) 451^{a}8–12, the possibility of wrongly regarding one's image as a copy; (*d*) 451^{a}12–14, the possibility of practising regarding it as a copy.

The reason why the person in situation (*a*) doubts whether he is remembering is that a memory-image needs to be 'in accordance with' (451^{a}4) a past perception, and he is unsure whether the accord exists. The reason why the person in situation (*c*) lacks memory is that a memory-image needs to be a copy and his is not.

For comment on the requirement that one's memory-image should be a copy of the thing remembered, see pp. 2–4. For Hume's somewhat different treatment of (*a*) doubt and (*c*) error as to whether one is remembering, see *A Treatise of Human Nature* I.III.V.

451ª3 'Do not know.' The doubt as to whether one is remembering may take the form of uncertainty as to whether one should regard one's image as a copy. (So it was suggested, on the basis of the phrase 'for this reason' (line 2) in the preceding note.) Judging now from line 4 (with note), it looks as if the reason for the doubt is that one is not sure whether one's image is 'in accordance with' a previous perception. One would suppose that in many cases, even if not in all, these uncertainties would prevent a man from regarding his image as a copy, or from saying in his soul that he encountered the imaged thing before, in other words from satisfying two of Aristotle's conditions for remembering. In such cases the doubt will then supply its own answer, namely that he is not remembering. At the same time, the doubt may constitute the only barrier to remembering. By simply setting it aside, he can, provided the other conditions are fulfilled, meet all Aristotle's conditions for remembering. (Indeed, it may be enough if he will regard his image as a copy, and say the right things in his soul, simply by way of experiment, or on the basis of evidence or testimony.) It seems improbable that Aristotle saw and accepted these surprising consequences. They cast doubt on his idea that regarding one's image as a copy, and being aware of a previous encounter, are necessary conditions of remembering.

One attempt at escape might be to say that the doubt concerns only whether one has memory, in the sense of an ability or tendency, and this doubt does not supply its own answer. However, this is an unlikely interpretation, since the words 'for this reason' in line 2, suggest that the discussion is going to be about regarding one's image as a copy, and hence about the act of remembering, not about the ability or tendency.

Another passage which suggests that, on Aristotle's principles, the doubt described here ought to resolve itself is 452ᵇ26–7, which says that one who is remembering cannot fail to notice that he is.

451ª4 'As a result of former perception . . . in accordance with the previous perception' (*apo tou aisthesthai proteron . . . kata to êisthêsthai*). 'In accordance with' cannot merely mean the same as 'as a result of'. It may refer to the requirement that in order for us to be remembering something we perceived, it is necessary that our image should be a copy of what we perceived, i.e. should be like it, as well as being 'a result of' it (see pp. 2–4). Or since the Greek phrase refers to the past act of perceiving, rather than to the thing perceived, it may imply the more stringent requirement that our present imagery should be a copy of *our past view of* the thing perceived.

451^{a}5–8 'At other times . . . ' This must introduce a new case. It is surely not intended to show how one can resolve the doubt described in lines 2–5.

451^{a}6 'Recollects.' This seems to be one of the two main types of recollection that Aristotle discusses (see p. 42). In this kind of case, one starts with an image of the thing one later recollects, but fails at first to refer the image to the thing. The aim of summoning up an image or images that are linked in a series with the starting image is to enable one to refer the starting image to the right thing. The other kind of case is probably not in Aristotle's mind here, because it does not involve an initial period of contemplating an image as something in its own right and a subsequent switch to regarding it as *of* another thing.

451^{a}14–15 'Memory and remembering.' See note on 449^{b}4.

451^{a}15–16 'Having' (*hexis*). Memory is a *hexis* in two senses (distinguished at *Metaph.* 1022^{b}4–12). First, it is the *having* of an image (450^{a}30; 451^{a}16. The cognate verb *echein*, 'to have', is used at 452^{a}11–12). Secondly, it is a certain kind of *state* (449^{b}25; 451^{a}23; 451^{a}27). At 451^{b}3, the word is used ambiguously as between 'having' and 'state'.

'Regarded as a copy of that of which it is an image.' Here again Aristotle does not seem to have in mind symbolic images. An image of the man, Coriscus, will be regarded as a copy, and so presumably is a copy, of Coriscus himself. It is not a copy of something that symbolizes Coriscus, for example of his hat. (See pp. 3–4.)

451^{a}16–17 'The primary perceptive part and that by which we perceive time.' The same thing, according to 450^{a}9–12. For further comment on the primary perceptive part (*to prôton aisthêtikon*), see notes on 449^{b}30; 450^{a}10–11; ^{a}11–12.

Notes to

CHAPTER TWO

451ª18 'Recollecting.' On the difference between recollecting and remembering, see Chapter 3.

451ª19–20 What is it that is to be taken as true? Not the conclusion that recollection is neither the recovery nor the acquisition of memory, for this is about to be proved, not assumed. It must be some of the premises in the proof that we are being asked to take as true. In that case, the word 'for' in 451ª20 will refer some way ahead to these premises.

'Essays' (*epicheirêmatikoi logoi*). The word is connected with the notion of an attempt. It is defined as dialectical reasoning (*Top.* 162ª16). (On dialectic, see pp. 27–31.) 'All that is true' emphasizes that perhaps not everything is. All this makes it unlikely that the reference is to chapter 1 above. Perhaps it is to essays, now lost, such as are listed in Diogenes Laertius' list of Aristotle's works.

The *De Memoria* does not make much use of the dialectical method of setting out from the opinions of others and so working towards a conclusion.

451ª20–1 'Recovery of memory.' Recollection is not this because (*a*) Recollection is the recovery of scientific knowledge, perception, etc. (451ᵇ2–5). So perception, the acquisition of knowledge, etc. must have preceded recollection. But it does not follow that memory has preceded, for perception, the acquisition of knowledge, etc. do not presuppose prior memory, nor do they incorporate within themselves the acquisition of memory, nor are they immediately followed by remembering. (This is the relevance of 451ª21–31, as was pointed out to me by Mr. Colin Lyas.) Since recollection is not always preceded by memory, it is not necessarily the recovery of memory.

Other reasons might also be given why, on Aristotle's principles, recollection is not the recovery of memory:

(*b*) Memory, in the sense of an ability or tendency, can exist up to the moment of recollection. (For it can precede recollection, see note on 451^{b}5–6, and can be retained during the recollective search, see note on 452^{a}7.) So to recollect is not necessarily to recover memory in this dispositional sense.

(c) Recollection cannot be defined simply as the recovery of memory, any more (see 451^{b}6–10) than it can be defined simply as the recovery of scientific knowledge, perception, etc., if we want to distinguish it from relearning.

Aristotle's aim in attacking the idea that recollection is the recovery of memory is not to correct anything in Plato. *Philebus* 34C says that the going over again of a lost memory can constitute recollection in certain circumstances. And *Phaedo* 73E suggests that recollection often involves prior forgetting. But Aristotle is not attacking the modest idea that memory sometimes precedes, and is sometimes recovered in recollection.

'Acquisition of memory.' That recollection is not simply this is argued in 451^{a}31–^{b}6, on the grounds that memory *can* be acquired before any act of recollection has taken place. This point in no way contradicts the earlier one that memory does not *have to* precede recollection.

The word 'for' in 451^{a}21 shows that what follows is meant to be relevant to the claim that recollection is not the recovery or acquisition of memory. This rules out the idea that Aristotle's main purpose in 451^{a}21–31 is to attack the theory of recollection of a former life in Plato's *Meno* and *Phaedo*.

451^{a}22–3 'Since none has preceded.' This reveals that Aristotle is excluding from consideration the case in which one learns something for the second time. He is thinking of learning something for the first time, and of having a kind of experience for the first time, or alternatively of having an experience that is particular, in the sense that one cannot have the very same one a second time. Consequently, in lines 21 and 25, we should be entitled to translate 'for the first time', instead of 'first'. Again in lines 29–31 when Aristotle speaks of a time-lapse, he will be thinking of a gap between learning or experiencing for the first time and remembering, or alternatively between having a non-repeatable experience and remembering.

451^{a}23–4 'State or affection' (*hexis* or *pathos*). Repeated ^{a}27–8. This is the phrase used at 449^{b}25 to define memory, i.e. the ability or tendency, not the act of remembering. There too there is insistence on a time-lapse. But here the requirement is made more precise. Not only is the state or affection subsequent to the original act of learning or experiencing, but even after the state or affection has been established, a further time-lapse is required before remembering starts.

Evidently, Aristotle is prepared, though with some misgivings, to say that the state or affection in some cases constitutes scientific knowledge (*epistêmê* 451ᵃ27-8), as well as memory, and it can constitute scientific knowledge from the start, without a pause for time to elapse.

We should distinguish (*a*) the initial act of experiencing or learning, (*b*) the resulting state or affection, which in some cases constitutes scientific knowledge, (*c*) this same state or affection after a further lapse of time, after which it constitutes memory. These distinctions are somewhat blurred in the Greek, since Aristotle uses the same Greek word *pathos* for the initial experience in (*a*)—451ᵃ24—and for the affection in (*b*) and (*c*).

451ᵃ25-31 'Further.' The further requirement is an extra time-lapse after the state or affection has been established, before remembering can start.

451ᵃ27 'If one should call...' Scientific knowledge (*epistêmê*) is a state (*NE* 1139ᵇ31), but Aristotle is worried at having suggested that it is an affection.

451ᵃ28 'Nothing prevents.' This second parenthetical comment refers to what follows. We are about to be told that a time-lapse is required before one can remember a piece of scientific knowledge. Aristotle now wants to reassure us that we are not prevented from remembering something of which we had scientific knowledge by (*a*) the fact that thought and memory are only incidentally connected with each other (450ᵃ13-14; ᵃ23-5) nor by (*b*) the fact that at the time we are actually exercizing our scientific knowledge of a proposition (and so contemplating the reasons why it is true, and deducing it from premises that state those reasons) we are not then said to be remembering it (449ᵇ17-18). Remembering it will involve simply thinking of the proposition itself, without deriving it from reasons.

451ᵃ28 'In virtue of an incidental association' (*kata sumbebêkos*).

The association between remembering and scientific knowledge is incidental for the same reasons as the association between memory and thought is incidental. These reasons are explained in the second note on 450ᵃ13–14.

451ᵃ29 'None the less remembering itself.' The contrast is with the affection and scientific knowledge, mentioned in ᵃ26–7, which can turn into memory only after a time-lapse, and the latter of which is only incidentally connected with memory.

451ᵃ29–31 'Until time has elapsed.' (Cf. 449ᵇ25.) The reason why this time-lapse is needed is revealed by the contrast between what one experienced earlier and what one experienced now. The use of the word 'now' suggests that an experience one has only just had will belong to the present, and so cannot yet be an object of memory, since memory is of the past.

The view that one does not yet remember what one has only just experienced, would be endorsed by those who postulate the so-called specious present (William James, *Principles of Psychology*, vol. I, pp. 605–48; Bertrand Russell, *The Analysis of Mind*, lecture IX.) For events contained in the rearward end of the specious present cannot yet be objects of genuine memory. The present which Aristotle envisages here has something in common with the specious present. For at any given instant, it has a certain span, and includes within itself experiences which one has just had. On the other hand, it is not clear that Aristotle has the idea of a specious present (on which see p. 21). For he omits to postulate such a thing in just those contexts where others have been tempted to do so, e.g. when he speaks of motion, change and the passage of time as objects of perception (*DA* 425ᵃ16; *Phys.* 219ᵃ3–4; note on *DM* 449ᵇ13–15), and again when he describes how one can estimate longer durations through one's knowledge of the shorter durations of certain mental processes (*DM* 452ᵇ17–22, with pp. 18–21).

Cf. *Phys.* 222ᵃ20–4 for the idea of a present which occupies a *stretch* of time.

451ᵃ31–ᵇ6 'Further' introduces the argument that recollection is not the acquisition of memory, since memory can be acquired before any recollection has taken place. 'From the start'—relatively speaking, in comparison with recollection, which presupposes a period during which something is lost and needs to be recovered. But the phrase should not be taken as withdrawing the requirement of a brief time-lapse before remembering starts.

451^{b}2-5 'The state connected with it' or 'The having of it'. *Hexis* is ambiguous as between these two. And the reference may be either to 449^{b}25 (memory is *a state connected with* perception or conception), or to 450^{a}30; 451^{a}16 (memory is *the having of* an image).

The recovery of perception will involve not perceiving again, but having an image of what was perceived. The recovery of scientific knowledge will not take the form of working out the scientific fact again from the reasons that make it so. For that would be to exercize scientific knowledge, not to recollect (cf. 449^{b}15-18). It will take the form simply of recovering the scientific fact and the reasons for it directly, without working anything out.

Plato had already connected recollection with the recovery of something. For he talks of the recovery of knowledge (*Meno* 85D; *Phaedo* 75E), of the recovery of something experienced (*Philebus* 34B-C), and of the going over again of a lost memory (ibid.).

Recovery implies loss. But what is it that is lost before recollection takes place? If I can recollect the dates of any English sovereign by simply thinking through the list of dates from 1066, we should not say that I lose my knowledge of the dates in between recollective performances. It is just that I probably won't think of the dates in between whiles. In other cases, however, recollection is achieved only after a great struggle. And here it may be reasonable to say that knowledge is temporarily lost, and recovered only through the effort of recollection. Plato had concentrated on cases of recollection where knowledge was temporarily lost (*Meno* 85C-D; 86A-C; *Phaedo* 73E; 74B-C; *Philebus* 34B-C). But Aristotle seems to be aware that one will not necessarily lose *dispositional* knowledge prior to recollection. For if the recollective search is going well, a man has the *ability* to move of his own accord on to the next image (452^{a}4-6). And Aristotle allows that in some cases one has memory at the time of the search (see note on 452^{a}7). Plato too acknowledges that it is not exclusively, but only 'especially', after forgetting that recollection occurs (*Phaedo* 73E).

451^{b}5-6 'When one does remember, it results that memory follows.' Aristotle is not using the word 'remember' (*mnêmoneuein*) carelessly to refer to recollecting, which would have been very confusing. On the contrary, the remembering here referred to is the remembering of line 451^{b}1, which precedes, and is contrasted with, recollecting. The aim of the sentence, as was pointed out to me by Professor Ackrill, is to connect the remembering (*mnêmoneuein*) of 451^{b}1 with the original formulations in terms of memory (*mnême*) at 451^{a}20; ^{a}22, ^{a}24. Not only can remembering (the act) precede any recollection, but also memory (the disposition) can precede any recollection, since it follows immediately on the remembering. Therefore the acquisition of memory can precede, and is not identical with, recollection.

451^{b}6 'These things'—scientific knowledge, perception, etc.

451^{b}9–10 'A principle which is over and above.' Both he who recollects and he who learns again have the power to learn. But the former has an additional power, which will finally be described in 452^{a}4–12. It turns out to be the power to move somehow through one's own agency from the starting-point on to what follows in a series of images. But before this can be made clear, we shall need an intervening discussion, which will explain what is meant by a series of images and a starting-point.

451^{b}11 'Change' (*kinêsis*). The change in question is an image. Aristotle is about to discuss the association of ideas or images which is involved in recollection. The word *kinesis* is ambiguous as between the process of change and the product of change. Aristotle uses it of the image (clear examples at 451^{a}3 and 452^{b}23). If the change is sometimes referred to as something persistent and not intermittent, this is because Aristotle sometimes thinks of the image this way (p. 16).

Aristotle concentrates on the kind of recollection that starts with the excitation of an image. He neglects the kind of recollection described in Plato's *Phaedo* 73C–74A, which starts with one *perceiving* something and thus being reminded of something else. However, the word translated 'change' could refer to this kind of perceptual process (450^{a}31), and so Aristotle could have used it to cover the sort of case envisaged in *Phaedo* 73C–74A, if he had had this sort of case in mind.

451^{b}11 'Nature' (the word is a cognate of *phusis*). Aristotle probably means that certain changes or images are naturally fitted to follow each other, for example images of things that are similar, opposite, or neighbouring to each other. But they may not follow each other regularly in fact, unless a suitable habit (*ethos* 451^{b}13) is established. We may compare how men are naturally fitted to acquire virtues, but will not in fact do so unless they make a habit of acting in a certain way (*NE* 1103^{a}23–6).

On another view, he means not merely that images are naturally *fitted* to follow each other, but that they do in fact follow each other regularly because of nature. But why then should he add that they follow each other because of habit (451^{b}13; 14; 18, 28)? For usually he distinguishes between what happens because of nature and what happens because of habit (*DM* 452^{a}27–8; ^{a}30–^{b}3; *Rhet.* 1370^{a}6–9; *NE* 1152^{a}29–31). Appeal may be made to *DM* 452^{a}30, which appears to allow that habit can result in nature. But it is doubtful that in the present passage Aristotle can mean that habit results in our images having a certain nature. For first, the kind of case in which habit results in nature is not the general rule (see note on 452^{a}30). And secondly, such a case would be more appropriately described by saying that habit results in *our* having a certain nature, rather than by saying that it results in our *images* doing so.

Why does not Aristotle mention artifice as well as nature? Mnemonists can make images occur in sequences as a result of artifice. The things imaged need not be similar, opposite, or neighbouring to each other. Nor are the images in any other way fitted by nature to occur in sequence. We need not suppose that Aristotle is forgetting these cases. His point may simply be that if there had not been cases of recollection occurring naturally, then there wouldn't have been any cases of recollection. When mnemonists employ the so-called artificial memory, this is a case of art imitating nature (*Phys.* 194^{a}21; 199^{a}15; *Meteor.* 381^{b}6).

For further comment, see p. 44–6.

451^{b}13 'Necessity' (*anankê*). This alternative is not mentioned again. Line 451^{b}28 pointedly drops it, saying that the changes follow each other by habit. Perhaps Aristotle mentions this alternative only for the sake of completeness, but can think of no examples. It is indeed difficult to think of any case in which one image invariably follows another. Someone may wish to maintain that in thinking of double, one necessarily thinks simultaneously of half. But this would not help, for Aristotle is talking of successive, not simultaneous, acts of thinking.

It does not help to point out that when Aristotle speaks of necessities he includes natural necessities along with logical ones. Nor would it help to suggest (what is probably untrue in any case, judging from the parallel between necessity and habit), that the necessity may be thought of as holding between the things imaged, and that there are plenty of examples of this, since premises and conclusion, or cause and effect, are linked by necessity. The trouble with these suggestions is that Aristotle clearly thinks of the images as invariably following each other in the case under consideration. And the suggestions do not help us to find any example of this.

451^{b}13 'Habit' (*ethos*). This word and its cognate, 'habituation' (*ethismos*), can refer first to repetitions such as often result in a tendency (*NE* 1179^{b}20–5). (Sometimes there is the implication that the repetitions succeed in producing the tendency (*NE* 1103^{a}20–1). But sometimes Aristotle speaks of unsuccessful habituation, in which the repetitions do not result in a tendency (*NE* 1103^{a}22).) The words can also refer secondly to a certain kind of tendency, regardless of whether it has been produced by repetition (*DM* 451^{b}14).

In 451^{b}13, the reference is probably, as it certainly is in the next line, to a certain kind of tendency, whether produced by repetition or not. Otherwise, Aristotle's opening remarks, in 451^{b}10–14, on the association of ideas, would neglect a large proportion of the cases. For, as lines 451^{b}14–16 point out, when images follow each other in sequence, this is not always the result of repetition.

The tendency that is a habit is opposed to necessity, and differs from it in admitting of more exceptions, and being subject to change (references in note on 452^{a}30).

Locke (*Essay Concerning Human Understanding* II.33) followed by Leibniz (*Nouveaux Essais sur l'Entendement Humain* II.33) was later to distinguish an association of ideas based on nature, one based on custom, and one based on a single strong impression. This threefold distinction has some affinity with Aristotle's, between an association due to necessity, one that is a habit due to repetitions, and one that is a habit due to a single experience. But the correspondence is not perfect.

The Greek at 451^{b}11–14 simply says 'if of necessity . . . but if not of necessity but by habit'. Aristotle means 'if the changes follow each other by habit', not 'if the changes are of a nature because of habit'. The former phrase becomes explicit at 451^{b}28. And in any case, the latter interpretation is ruled out in the note on 'Nature', 451^{b}11.

Habit is to be found only where there is regularity. But one may make an unwonted move from one image to another. This will not be due to habit, and may even be contrary to habit. It can result from a relationship between the things one is imaging. For example, if two names are very similar to each other, one may blunder on to the wrong one, when one is trying to recollect a man's name (452^{a}30–^{b}6). Here similarity has influenced the order of one's ideas, but habit has played no part.

For further comment, see pp. 45–6.

451^{b}16 'Then.' Having explained in 451^{b}10–16 what makes recollection possible, Aristotle is now in a position to explain the manner in which it occurs.

He attaches importance to the image that corresponds to the *penultimate* item in a series, throughout the passage (see 451^{b}18; 451^{b}21–2; 451^{b}31; 452^{a}9–10). Why? The main reason is that in 451^{b}18–22 he concentrates on a particularly favourable case of recollection. This is a case in which one's starting-point is such as to lead one straight on to the thing one wishes to recollect. But 'for the most part' (451^{b}24), one will pass through a number of other images, which come earlier than this ('other' *heterôn* 451^{b}24; 'earlier' *proterôn* 451^{b}17; 'distant' *porrhô* 451^{b}26). In such cases, it is not till one reaches the image that corresponds to the penultimate item in the series that one will be in a position to move straight on to the thing one wishes to recollect. Hence the interest in the image of this penultimate item.

The image corresponding to the penultimate item in the series would have additional importance in the kind of case envisaged at 451^{a}6 (see note). For it is on arriving at this image that one is able at last to refer the image that one started with to the right thing.

It is with a view to cutting out the earlier images, and taking a short cut ('this is exactly why' 451^{b}18; 'therefore' 451^{b}23), that one sometimes specially chooses a starting-point that will lead one straight on to the thing one wishes to recollect. The method for taking a short cut is to start in one's thoughts from something similar, opposite, or neighbouring to the thing one wishes to recollect. If someone wishes to recollect what he did last Tuesday, he may start in his thoughts from what he did last Monday, which is neighbouring. Then, with any luck, the image corresponding to this thing will come next to, or overlap with, or even be the same as, the image of the thing to be recollected (451^{b}18–22). Similar, opposite, and neighbouring are relations that hold between the things imaged.

But even when one does not take a short cut, the method of recollecting is still in principle the same ('like those we spoke of' *hoiôn* 451^{b}25; 'the method is the same' 451^{b}27), if one considers the relation of each item in the series to its successor, and, most importantly, the relation of the penultimate item in the series to its successor.

451^{b}19 'From the present or from something else.' The reference is to the temporal status of the imaged thing, not to that of the image, for one cannot help starting from a present image. In some cases, the imaged things will not have temporal positions (as milk, white, mist, fluid, autumn do not). And then there will be no question of starting from the present, assuming (see note on 451^{b}11 'change') that Aristotle does not have in mind the kind of case envisaged in Plato's *Phaedo* 73C–74A, where the sight of e.g. milk (which is in sight now) leads to the recollection of something else.

451^{b}19–20 'Similar . . . opposite . . . neighbouring.' i.e. to the thing we wish to recollect. For full comment, see pp. 42–6.

The reference is still to relations between things imaged. Aristotle is describing a special case of recollection, in which one takes a short cut. One seeks out (451^{b}22–3; ^{b}27–8) something similar, opposite, or neighbouring to the thing one wishes to recollect, and, with any luck, one will be led directly from the thought of this thing to the recollection of what one was seeking. The relation of neighbouring can be temporal or spatial.

A problem may be raised. If one has not yet recollected something, how can one yet know enough about it to know what will be similar, opposite, or neighbouring to it? This is like the problem raised in Plato's *Meno* 80D. The answer is that one always knows some answer to the question, 'What are you seeking?', and this knowledge should enable one to think of something similar, opposite, or neighbouring-to the thing sought.

451^{b}20–1 'The changes connected with these things' *(hai kinêseis toutôn)*. i.e. the images connected with the things. For the phrase, cf.

450^b27-8; 452^a1-2; 452^b23. Aristotle here turns from the relation between things imaged to the relation between images, and explains why, in the special case under consideration, one will be led directly from one's starting-point to recollection of the thing sought.

Some commentators try to correlate the object which is similar and the image which is the same, the object which is neighbouring and the image which includes a part, the object which is opposite and the image which is together. But this requires excessive ingenuity. It is simpler to suppose that no such neat correlation is intended. The point is merely that if we start from an image of something that is similar, opposite, or neighbouring, it will (with any luck) come next to, or overlap with, or even be the same as, the image of the thing to be recollected.

Suppose, for example, I want to recollect where I put my hammer. I think of something neighbouring, namely, putting away my chisel. This action was neighbouring in time, since I put the chisel away just before I put away the hammer. The memory-image I now have of putting away the chisel, and the sense-image I originally had of putting away the chisel, may portray me putting away the hammer as well as the chisel. In this case, a single image will enable me to recollect ('in some cases are the same'). Alternatively, the image of my stowing away the chisel may finish by showing the beginning of my stowing away the hammer ('in others include a part'). Aristotle is thinking of a temporal overlap, an overlap in the original sense-images when he says 'the remainder which one underwent after that part is small'. The third alternative is that the image of stowing the chisel and the image of stowing the hammer occurred as sense-images, and will recur as memory-images, one next to the other in time ('in others are together'). Just as the original actions were 'neighbouring' in time, so the corresponding images are 'together' in time.

The method could work for spatial as well as for temporal relations. If I want to recollect how one portion of the garden looks, I may form an image of a neighbouring portion. This image may enable me to transfer my mental gaze uninterruptedly across to the adjacent portion of garden, or may already portray some, or all, of that portion.

It is noteworthy that Aristotle allows that one and the same image can represent two different items ('in some cases are the same').

451^{b}23 'But also when they do not search in this way they recollect.'
Does 'in this way' go with 'search' or with 'recollect'? The translation omits any comma, so as to leave it ambiguous. In either case,
the point that Aristotle is going on to make is that people for the
most part do not take the short cut described in 451^{b}18–22 and
specially seek out a starting point that will be similar, opposite, or
neighbouring, to the thing they wish to recollect. ('They do not
search [in this way]'.) Rather they pass through a chain of earlier
images, before they reach such a point. But even by the longer
method they still recollect, and indeed recollect in the same manner.
('[In this way] they recollect'.) The manner is the same, if one
considers the relation of each item in the series to its successor.

To take 'in this way' with 'search' is more strain on the Greek.
But it may make the sense a little bit clearer.

On either interpretation, Aristotle is not here bringing up the
idea that people may recollect, without having deliberately sought
for the thing they wish to recollect. What they omit to seek for is the
special kind of starting point described in 451^{b}18–22. This fits best
with the sense of the passage.

The *De Memoria* nowhere else mentions the possibility of people
recollecting without having deliberately sought for the thing they
wish to recollect. (453^{a}17–20 does not describe such a case.) On the
other hand, that there should be such cases is not ruled out by the
statement that recollection is a search (453^{a}15; cf. ^{a}25) since this
needs to be understood in the light of the more guarded statement
that it is, as it were, a kind of search (453^{a}12). More damaging to the
idea that the *De Memoria* allows recollection without search is the
fact that it denies recollection to lower animals, on the grounds that
recollection is too intellectual a process (453^{a}6–14). It is surprising
that Aristotle does not here mention recollection without search,
and more surprising if he means to exclude it, since it is recollection
without search that Plato seems to have in mind in *Phaedo* 73C–74A.
And Aristotle's discussion is inspired in some respects by the *Phaedo*.
Moreover, the *Nicomachean Ethics* speaks of recollection without
search, in connexion with wicked men who are reminded of unpleasant things against their wills (1166^{b}15). Aristotle comes closer
to discussing examples of this type, though without using the name
'recollection' in *Insom.* 460^{b}3–16. See pp. 40–1.

451^{b}24–5 'For the most part . . . other changes like those we spoke of.' For the most part, we have to go through longer chains, in which there are 'other' images before the penultimate one. In what way are the images in these longer chains 'like' the ones already spoken of? Is it that an image and its successor follow each other by habit? Or is it that they will be images of things similar, opposite, or neighbouring to each other? In the latter case, we are free to suppose that such relations hold in the longer chains only 'for the most part'.

451^{b}26–7 'Distant ... neighbouring ... the method is the same.' The word 'neighbouring' here bears a weaker sense than at 451^{b}20, since it means only adjacent in the order of thinking, not neighbouring in the order of occurrence in the real world. When there are 'other' images to go through before the penultimate one, the item we finally remember will be 'distant' from the item we start with, because of the intervening images. The method is still the same, however, as when one's chain of images is short (which it is in the short cut described at 451^{b}18–22, and perhaps in other cases too). The only respect of sameness explicitly mentioned is that the images follow each other by habit. Nothing obliges us to suppose that Aristotle means that in all recollection an item is similar, opposite, or neighbouring to its successor (neighbouring, as at 451^{b}20, in the order of occurrence in the real world).

The series described here as extending into the distance may well be a series like that at 451^{b}19, which starts from something present and travels into the past.

451^{b}27–8 The mss. here have a strange jumble of words (deleted by Freudenthal, followed by W. D. Ross) which may well be a gloss not written by Aristotle: 'I mean (or he means) the successor, not having searched in advance, and not having recollected.' Could the words originally have meant that, when the thing to be remembered is distant, a man uses the same method in the sense that he moves from a given item to a *successor* that is similar, opposite or neighbouring? He does not, however, like the person in 451^{b}18–22 'search out in advance' a starting point that is similar, opposite, or neighbouring to the thing to be recollected.

This interpretation of the phrase 'not having searched in advance' fits with the interpretation we put on the phrase 'and when they do not search' or 'and when they do not search in this way' (451^{b}23). We took this as meaning: when people do not specially seek out a starting-point that is similar, opposite, or neighbouring to the thing to be recollected.

The use of the word 'successor' brings out two points. In 451^b18–22, the man who takes a short cut is described as moving from a predecessor (451^b19) that is similar, opposite, or neighbouring, directly to the thing he wishes to recollect. But in the case considered here, a move does not necessarily take one to the thing one wishes to recollect, but only to the next item in the series, whatever that may be. Hence a reference to the successor rather than to the thing one wishes to recollect. Secondly, the move is better described, not as a move *from* something similar, opposite, or neighbouring, but rather as a move *to* something similar, opposite, or neighbouring. Hence the reference to a successor rather than to a predecessor.

451^b29 'Thus.' i.e. because of the importance of the penultimate image, one will try to get a starting-point for reaching this penultimate image. By 'a starting-point for a change after which . . . ' Aristotle means, 'a starting-point for reaching a change'. And he means, 'a change after which', not 'a starting-point after which.' (The latter would be to recommend the short cut procedure of 451^b18–22. But now he evidently has in mind cases in which one passes through a longer chain of images).

451^b30 'A starting-point' (*archê*). All recollection has to start somewhere. So when Aristotle says that recollections are achieved quickest and best from a starting-point, one would expect him to mean not any kind of starting-point, but some special kind.

Lines 452^a1–2 suggest two restrictions. Aristotle seems to be thinking of a starting-point in a series in which the items 'are related to each other in succession', and in which the images follow the order of the things. Not all associated items meet these conditions. For example, the students in a class may be associated by contiguity, but they will not necessarily be related to each other in any particular order or succession. Again, sometimes images are given an order by artifice, e.g. by use of the place system, and the images impose order on the items memorized, rather than following the order of these items. Would Aristotle therefore say that one is not using a starting-point of the relevant kind, when one starts from the first in a series of mnemonic places, or when one seeks the name of a student in a class by thinking of the names of other students? It seems surprising that he should intend such tight restrictions. And indeed, on one interpretation, lines 452ᵃ12–13 imply that the user of a place-system does begin from a starting-point of the relevant kind.

There is a further puzzle, in that the distinction drawn between recollecting and relearning at 452ᵃ4–6 seems to imply that all recollecting involves a starting-point, whereas lines 451ᵇ31–452ᵃ1 suggest that only the quickest and best recollection begins from a starting-point.

On one interpretation, lines 452ᵃ7–10 supply an example of a man whose search does not begin from a starting-point. He is described as 'exciting many changes' in the effort to recollect. Perhaps he has not reached a starting-point at the time when he is stirring up these images. In that case, either he will recollect without using a starting-point at all, or he will eventually reach a starting-point, though his search will not have begun from one.

We are given some examples of starting-points. One would be the first step in a mathematical proof (452ᵃ3). Another would be the first item in the series, milk, white, air, fluid, autumn (452ᵃ14–16). And again the middle member of a triplet of memorized items can be used as a starting point (452ᵃ17–24).

451ᵇ31 'And this is why.' Because, given a starting-point, one will be led to the all-important penultimate image.

452ᵃ1–2 'For as the things are related to each other in succession, so also are the changes.' Aristotle is not saying that the things always have an order of their own, nor that the images always follow the order of the things. This would be false (see pp. 44–5, and note on 451ᵇ30).

There is an ambiguity in the notion of the order of the images. In the method of mid-points described at 452ᵃ17–24, the images were originally arranged in a certain order in the mind, but they can be summoned up in a different order.

452ᵃ3 'Order' (*taxis*). Things related as similar, opposite, or neighbouring will not necessarily be related in a particular order (see note on 451ᵇ30). The students in a class need not have an order. So the importance of order is an additional point. Its importance was stressed in other treatments of mnemonics, e.g. by the Pythagoreans, according to Iamblichus, *Life of Pythagoras* 164–6, printed in Diels, *Die Fragmente der Vorsokratiker*, and by Cicero, *De Oratore* II. 86, 353; 354; 359.

452ᵃ4 The distinction between recollecting and relearning, mentioned in 451ᵇ6-10, can at last be drawn, now that the idea has been introduced of a series of images and a starting-point in such a series. The main difference from relearning is that one who recollects does not depend on someone else. Without such help he will be able to move from the starting-point on to what comes next. One who is relearning something, e.g. a mathematical proof (cf. 452ᵃ3), may be like the recollector in having to move from a starting-point to the next step in a series (see pp. 38–40). But he will differ in depending on someone else's help.

Aristotle is wrong, or at least misleading, in his statements about learning and about recollection, where Plato had been right on both counts. For a discussion, see pp. 37–40. In saying that the recollector does not depend on someone else, he is following part of Plato's account, and even repeating some of Plato's phraseology. But he does not pay attention, as Plato does, to the extent to which memory-jogging is permissible.

In implying that the relearner does depend on someone else, he is neglecting Plato's insight that a person can learn, and can relearn, something through his own agency, and without depending on someone else. Why does he neglect it? Steven Tigner has argued, in a paper as yet unpublished, that for the Greeks there was a strong temptation to think of learning as involving being taught by someone else. (Thus the verb 'to learn' is paraphrased as 'to receive knowledge', Plato *Euthydemus* 277B; Aristotle *DA* 417ᵇ12. Again, Meno sometimes assumes that what can be learnt can be taught (Plato, *Meno* 70A), and an absence of teachers from whom one learns is sometimes taken to imply an absence of learners (*Meno* 96B–C).) Perhaps we can partly explain the fact to which Tigner has pointed, by saying that when one gains knowledge, without being taught by someone else, the Greeks find it somewhat more natural to speak of discovering, not of learning. At any rate, Plato on the whole prefers to describe the slave boy as discovering, not learning. And for some kind of contrast between discovery and learning, see Archytas, fragment 3, in Diels, *Die Fragmente der Vorsokratiker*; Plato, *Cratylus* 436A, 438A–B, 439B; *Phaedo* 85C; *Laches* 186E; Aristotle *DA* 429ᵇ9.

452ᵃ7 'He no longer remembers.' This suggests that one does have memory in at least some of the cases where the recollective search is going smoothly, and where one can move forward without help, from the starting-point. And indeed, if memory is, with certain qualifications, the power to excite the right image (452ª10-11), one would expect this power to be retained in many cases, provided that it did exist at some earlier stage. Admittedly, memory and the power to excite the right image can be lost before recollection takes place, and they are sometimes regained only through the effort of recollection. For example, one may no longer remember what one did last Tuesday, and recapture memory only by a process of recollection. The case envisaged at 452ª7-10 is probably one in which memory either did not exist, or was lost, before recollection. But the case is described only as happening 'often'. And this implies that it does not happen always.

452ª7 'Often.' Is this man unable to reach a starting-point, or unable to move on to what follows it? In either case, he will suffer a temporary loss of memory. For both the man who cannot move through his own agency on to what follows the starting-point (452ª7) and the man who does not have the power to excite the right image (452ª10-12) lack memory.

452ª10 'For remembering . . .' 'For' explains the reference to remembering in 452ª7. The remembering in question is the ability or tendency, not the act. It has earlier been called a state or affection (*hexis* or *pathos* 449b25; 451ª23-4; ª27-8). The affection has turned out to be a sort of imprinted image (450ª27-b20). And now it appears that the state is the ability to stir up the image. Thus memory is both a stat e and an affection.

452ª12 'And this is why.' Either: it is thought to be on account of the need for a starting-point that people recollect starting from mnemonic places (for in the place-system, one has ready access to a starting-point). Or: on account of their having a starting-point and consequently going quickly, people are sometimes wrongly thought to be using that special device for increasing speed, viz. the place-system.

452ª13 'Places' (*topoi*). See pp. 22-31. The example given in 452ª14-16 probably does not illustrate the use of places. For the special value of the place-system is that, thanks to the contiguity of the images, one can memorize in a given order a set of items that have no memorable relationship of their own, for example a set of fifty names chosen at random. The items mentioned at 452ª14–16, however, do have a relationship of their own. For adjacent items in the series, milk, white, air, fluid, autumn, are similar to each other. Or if Aristotle agrees with e.g. the Hippocratic treatise, *On the Nature of Man*, that autumn is a dry season, the last two items on the list will be associated by contrast. And possibly white and air are associated not because mist is white, but because air bubbles produce the whiteness of foam, and of many other stuffs (*GA* 735ª30–736ª22; 784ᵇ15; 786ª7–13).

We can imagine that the person described is trying to recollect e.g. what is the next subject referred to in some poem, and that the answer is that the subject is autumn.

452ª13 'The reason is.' Either: the reason why one should get a starting-point. Or: the reason why those who have got one are thought (wrongly) to be using the place-system.

452ª17 'In every case the middle.' Not 'the middle of everything', i.e. of the whole series. For Aristotle is going on to discuss the middle of each triplet in the series, not the middle of the whole series. See pp. 31–4 for the explanation of this passage.

'In every case' is an exaggeration. He should say 'in all series of a certain kind', or 'in every batch in the series'.

'The middle also.' i.e. as well as the end, which served as the starting-point in the example just given in 452ª14–16.

452ª17–18 'For if no sooner, a person will remember when he comes to this.' i.e. if not at Θ, one will remember (provided the thing sought is associated with the first triplet along) when he comes to the middle of the first triplet.

452ª19 ΑΒΓΔΕΖΗΘ are images (see p. 31). The reason for thinking that they are images is that if they were something else, for example if they were the names of months in the year, it would be hard to skip about in the series in the way that Aristotle prescribes. The 'things denoted by ΑΒΓΔΕΖΗΘ' are the things for which the images stand.

452ª21; ª25–6 'He can move;' 'It is possible to move.' This shows that Aristotle does not think of one as surveying the whole triplet with a single glance. Rather one first looks at the middle member, and then shifts one's glance to the neighbouring members.

452ª22–3 One is seeking H, E, Δ, or B, because one is seeking the things they stand for.

452ª27 'Something old.' The sense required is: something less familiar (in contrast with the thing to which one is more habituated). This sense can be obtained, whichever of several ms. readings we adopt. If 'old' be read, interpret: faint and worn, and so unfamiliar. If 'not old' be read, interpret: not ingrained, hence unfamiliar. A third ms. reading can mean either: what has not lately been traversed, and so is unfamiliar, or what was not originally traversed, and so is unfamiliar. In fact, the first reading is best, because 450ᵇ4 has ready introduced us to the idea of old surfaces wearing down.

'Something to which one is more habituated.' i.e. something more customary, as a sequel, not in itself. Aristotle does not have in mind a case in which one habit (the habit of thinking of some single thing, R) interferes with another (the habit of thinking of the sequence, Q after P). Rather he has in mind a case in which a habit (the habit of thinking of the sequence, Q after P) interferes with recollection.

'For.' That habit has the force of nature explains why one moves to something to which one is more habituated.

452ª28 'And this is why.' It is best to take this parenthesis as continuing until 452ª30. For then 'frequency' in ª30 can pick up 'frequently' in ª28. And 'the activity' in ª30 will be supplied with a reference (namely the activity of thinking of something and of recollecting, mentioned in ª28–9).

Aristotle is again discussing not a habit of thinking of some single thing, but a habit of thinking of things in a certain order. His idea is that once we have a habit of thinking of B after A, we will recollect B quickly. And this is because habit is like nature. Thus in nature, events of kind B tend to follow events of kind A, and where this is so, an event of kind B will follow quickly on the occurrence of an event of kind A. Similarly, if we have a habit of thinking of B after A, we will recollect B quickly once we have thought of A. Indeed, not only is habit like nature in this way, but habit can actually produce in us a second nature, so that it comes to be second nature to think of B after A.

452ª30 'The activity.' sc. of thinking of something and of recollecting (452ª28–9).

452ᵃ30 'Frequency creates nature.' This is the opinion of Evenus (*NE* 1152ᵃ31) and of the author of the *Magna Moralia* (1203ᵇ30–2). Cf. also Plato, *Republic* 395D. In such a case, will the resulting tendency be both habitual and natural? If so, such cases cannot be the general rule, since in Aristotle's view habit is merely similar to nature. It differs from nature in admitting of more exceptions, and in being easier to change (*DM* 452ᵃ27–8; ᵃ30–ᵇ3; *Rhet.* 1370ᵃ6–9; *NE* 1152ᵃ29–31). This implies that the class of the habitual cannot overlap very extensively with the class of the natural.

452ᵃ30 'But just as . . .' In the previous example, it was habit that diverted one to the wrong destination. But in the next example one is diverted by similarity, working against (452ᵇ2) habit. Whenever images follow each other regularly, habit is at work. And this habit may be formed under the influence of some similarity between the things imaged. But where images follow each other, not in the regular order, but in an unwonted order, the sequence is not a habitual one. The order may none the less be influenced by some similarity between the things imaged. And this is what happens here. See pp. 45–6.

When similarity associates two or more names together, one can be led to the wrong name without travelling via the right one.

If we follow W. D. Ross' text, Aristotle has here, as often elsewhere, started the sentence with 'Since' (which I have not translated) and has left an anakolouthon. I have left out a similar 'Since' at 449ᵇ30.

452ᵇ1 In the realm of natural events, we do not find luck (*tuchê*), but if anything, only what Aristotle calls spontaneity (*to automaton*), *Phys.* 197ᵇ32–7. But Aristotle speaks of luck, because this is commoner than spontaneity in the realm of habitual events, which he is going to mention next. For the distinction between luck and spontaneity, see *Phys.* II. 6.

452ᵇ2 'Still more is this so.' i.e. still more is it so that there occur events contrary to *habit* and the result of luck. Aristotle means that the events are contrary to habit, not to nature, for in the example given of a man who blunders on to the wrong name, the occurrence is not contrary to nature. Rather it is in accordance with nature, because the wrong name is similar to the right one, and this creates a natural link between the images of these names (see pp. 44–6).

'Seeing that . . . ' The argument is that events that are due to habit do not enjoy the regularity of nature, but admit of more exceptions.

452^{b}5–6 'Blunder': *soloikizomen* (cf. English 'solecism'). The men of Soloi spoke bad Greek.

452^{b}7 This evidently concludes the discussion of the *manner* of recollection. More will be said about recollection later. But the next portion, on judging temporal distances, applies to all remembering, whether it be the result of recollection, or not. As to how we judge temporal distances, see pp. 18–21. Aristotle had in his lecture room a white board, on which he could display diagrams, such as the following, to his audience, if we may believe Henry Jackson, 'Aristotle's Lecture-room and Lectures', *The Journal of Philology*, 1920.

452^{b}7 'Units of measurement.' e.g. the day before yesterday (see 453^{a}1).

452^{b}11 'Some people.' Plato and Empedocles, according to *DS* 437^{b}10–438^{a}5.

452^{b}13–15 'Larger things . . . smaller things.' i.e. (*a*) 'How does thinking of large external objects differ from thinking of small external objects? It differs because ('for' 452^{b}14) the small-scale representations within will be correspondingly large or small, to match the external objects.'

The reading adopted here, and this interpretation of it, fits best with Aristotle's general theme. For he is concerned at first with estimating *relative* sizes. Thus he opens with a remark about judging *more* and *less* time. And the mental diagram described below provides a way of estimating *two* time periods, one by means of its relation to the other. We should expect his interest here then to be in thinking about the relative sizes of larger and smaller external objects. We should therefore reject interpretation (*b*): 'How does thinking of external objects differ from contemplating small-scale internal representations? It doesn't differ at all, because ('for' 452^{b}14) the small-scale representations are proportioned to match the external objects.'

452^{b}15–16 'Perhaps just as one can receive in oneself something distinct but in proportion to the forms, so also in the case of the distances.' The forms in question are the so-called sensible forms, e.g. the colour, shape, and size of the objects perceived. The reference is not to the intelligible forms which the mind separates out from within the sensible forms.

In perception, the sense-organs receive the sensible forms of the external objects. The eye-jelly, for example, can take on not only colours, but also shapes and sizes, in that the coloured patches in the eye-jelly can have certain shapes and sizes. What Aristotle usually says is that the organ receives the very same form (i.e. the same universal, not the same instance of it) as resides in the external object, and not a merely analogous form. Why then does he here speak as if the thing received is distinct and merely proportioned to match the form? There are two reasons. (i) In the case of magnitudes this is inevitable, because one can perceive magnitudes far larger than is one's eye-jelly. The eye-jelly cannot accommodate colour patches as large as this, but can only receive small-scale equivalents. (See Hintikka, 'Aristotelian Infinity', *The Philosophical Review*, 1966.) (ii) In any case, Aristotle is concerned here with thinking, not with perceiving. And one thinks not by means of the sensible forms received into the sense-organs, but by means of images left behind by these forms. The images may have colours, shapes and sizes not identical with, but only analogous to, those which were originally received.

The thing proportioned to match the distances, which Aristotle mentions in line 16, is evidently an image. For he goes on to speak of it as 'the change connected with the time'. He puts it on a level with the 'change connected with the thing', and the latter is certainly an image.

452^b16–17 'The distances.' The mental diagram described below could be used for calculating spatial distances more easily than for calculating temporal ones. And Aristotle probably has in mind both spatial and temporal ones. He has shown an interest in spatial distances at 452^b10 ('distant' and 'stretching'). But for the discussion of memory, the important question is how to calculate temporal distances. And it is with this that pages 18–21 above are concerned. These pages should be consulted for details of the procedure.

452^b21 'BE.' If one wants to know about two time periods, then one will need to think of AB as well as BE. But one need not make a mental movement along both lines. It will suffice if one makes a mental movement along BE, and from its duration calculates the length of one time period. One can then get the length of the other time period from knowledge of the relative lengths of the two periods.

452^{b}23–4 'The change connected with the thing and that connected with the time.' Not (a) two parts of the diagram just described, but (b) the diagram just described, which is connected with the time, and the image described in chapter 1, and there referred to as a change (kinêsis 451^{a}3), which is an image of the thing remembered. (This was pointed out to me by Miss Jeannette Desor.) Evidence: (i) unless Aristotle had in mind (b), he would hardly suppose (452^{b}28–9) that the absence of either one of the two changes mentioned is enough to prevent one from remembering. (ii) Provided he means (b), there is a reasonably common mistake for him to be referring to when he says (452^{b}24), 'if one thinks one is doing this, when one is not'. Moreover, the mistake is one he has mentioned before. See next note.

452^{b}24–5 'If a person thinks he is doing this, when he is not, then he thinks he is remembering.' There is a mistake which is common enough to be worth referring to, and which moreover has been mentioned before. One may wrongly suppose that one's image is a copy of a certain thing, i.e. is derived from it and is similar to it. (Cf. 451^{a}2–5; ^{a}8–12, for this mistake.) In certain cases (see footnote 3 on p. 3), this will result in wrongly supposing that one's image is an image of that thing. And if one is wrong in making that supposition, then in the terminology of the present passage, one will be wrong in supposing one has a change (kinêsis) connected with that thing.

452^{b}26–9 'Turned out to be.' See 449^{b}22–3; ^{b}28–9; 450^{a}18–21; 450^{b}20–451^{a}2; 451^{a}5–8. Aristotle is in fact wrong in supposing that, when remembering, one must be aware that one is, and must be aware of the time-lapse. 451^{a}2–5 unwittingly violates this principle. See p. 10 with footnote 1.

452^{b}30 'Of two sorts.' For the distinction, cf. William James, Principles of Psychology, 1890, vol. 1, p. 631.

453^{a}5 'In what precedes' 449^{b}6–8. The difference is due to the different kind of physiological conditions required for successful performance in the two cases (see note on 449^{b}7–8). The distinction between recollecting and remembering is timely, because the main discussion of recollection has just been interrupted by a discussion of estimating time-lapses, which is involved in all remembering. This last discussion speaks only of remembering, and does not use the verb for recollecting.

453^{a}7 'The time.' Remembering can occur without a substantial time gap after the original perception, learning, or experience. Recollection cannot (451^{a}31–^{b}6).

453^{a}10 'A sort of reasoning.' This makes it all the harder to distinguish recollection from relearning (see pp. 39–40). Later, Leibniz was to claim that the association of ideas provides only a shadow of reasoning, while Hume was to respond that there is no reasoning concerning matters of fact distinct from the association of ideas (see pp. 42–3). *Sullogismos* (reasoning) is not confined to syllogistic reasoning.

453^{a}12–14 'For indeed' is difficult. The thought may go as follows. 'This kind of search is found only in animals that can deliberate. This confirms that recollection is a sort of reasoning, for deliberation is a sort of reasoning.'

'The deliberating part.' A loose way of referring to the power to deliberate (cf. note on 450^{a}16–17). For Aristotle's account of deliberation, see *NE* 1112^{a}18–1113^{a}14. Where I have written 'part', the Greek has no noun. I have supplied a noun which could, like the Greek phrase, refer to the body as well as to the soul, though here the intended reference is to a power of the soul.

453^{a}14 'Something to do with the body.' Plato *Philebus* 34B–C had maintained that in recollection the soul acts on its own without the aid of the body. Further, Aristotle has just argued that recollection is a rather intellectual process, which might, given Aristotle's views (*DA* 403^{a}8), seem to support the idea that recollection is not dependent on the body. Consequently, Aristotle devotes the last section of the *De Memoria* to refuting the idea.

453^{a}15–16 'A search in something bodily for an image.' The image is in the body, because (*a*) it is in the soul (450^{b}10–11; 451^{a}3), and the soul is in the body (450^{a}29); (*b*) every mental occurrence can be said in some sense to 'be' a physiological process which is in the body (*DA* 403^{a}3–^{b}19), though it is not simply a physiological process. The part of the body in question is the heart.

453ᵃ16 'A sign.' If people get upset, and if after giving up they succeed in recollecting (or if after giving up they continue to be upset), why should these facts provide a sign that recollection is something to do with the body? They provide a sign because of the explanation they point to. The explanation of the facts is that in recollecting, one sets up a motion which is in some cases hard to stop 453ᵃ20–5 (hence the upset, and hence the upset's continuing after one has given up). The motion will continue until the thing sought is recollected 453ᵃ25–6 (hence the eventual success after giving up).

453ᵃ16 'It upsets some people.' Cf. Diogenes of Apollonia, according to Theophrastus, *De Sensibus*, sec. 45.

453ᵃ18 'And when they are no longer trying, they recollect none the less.' Or: 'And when they are no longer trying to recollect, it upsets them no less.' No doubt, Aristotle believes both these propositions. For if the upset continues after they have given up trying, this is because the motion they have set up continues, and this motion will go on continuing until they succeed in recollecting. Conversely, if they succeed in recollecting after they have given up trying, this will be because the motion they have set up has continued, and the prolongation of this motion is what causes the upset.

In allowing the possibility of recollecting after giving up, Aristotle is not going back on his statements that recollection must be through one's own agency (452ᵃ4–6), and that it is, as it were, a kind of search (453ᵃ12).

453ᵃ19 'Melancholic people.' The name does not indicate sadness, nor melancholia in the modern sense. Greek: *melancholikoi*, from the words for black bile. Theories differed as to whether the cause of melancholy was the mere presence of black bile in the body, or its presence in excess, or its presence in a particular place, or in a particular state, or from a particular source, or something unconnected with black bile. See *Probl.* XXX.1 for a Peripatetic view on this question.

Getting upset, and recollecting after giving up (or remaining upset after giving up) all result from setting up a motion that is hard to stop. Presumably then all these things are here being attributed to melancholics.

A problem arises because at 453ᵃ23 Aristotle says that those who get upset most are those who have fluid around the perceptual organs, while at 453ª18–19 he implies that it is melancholics who get upset most. Does Aristotle think of melancholics as having fluid around the perceptual organs? If so, this may seem surprising, because it was a common view that melancholy was connected with dryness (see the Hippocratic treatises *On the Nature of Man* 7; 15; *Aphorisms* III.14; *Airs, Waters, Places* 10). This view was shared by the author of the pseudo-Aristotelian *Problems* I.12. (See also *Problems* XXX.1, 954ª7, which describes melancholics as having hard bodies.) At a later date, the connexion between melancholy and dryness was asserted by Rufus of Ephesus and by Galen, and consequently by most subsequent theorists. The best solution is probably to suppose that in Aristotle's view melancholy arises when the black bile fluid, dry and sticky as it is, settles in the region of the heart. It was at any rate Diocles' view (fragment 42 in Wellman, *Fragmentsammlung der Griechischen Aerzte*, vol. 1) that melancholy resulted from the action of black bile around the heart, and Diocles was a pupil of Aristotle in the opinion of Werner Jaeger (*Diocles von Karystos*, Berlin, 1938; also *The Philosophical Review*, 1940).

Other pertinent characteristics of melancholics. They are impetuous, and don't wait to identify things, or to reason, or deliberate, but simply follow their imagination. They have long strings of images, and move quickly from one to the next. They go at it hard, and get excited, and form strong desires. (*Div.* 463ᵇ15–22; 464ª32–ᵇ5; *NE* 1150ᵇ25–7; 1152ª19; 1154ᵇ13; *Probl.* 903ᵇ19–20). This fits in well with what we are told about them here. That they have long strings of images fits in with the fact that they go through a prolonged recollective search, which they cannot stop. That they are excitable fits in with their getting upset. That they are too impetuous to deliberate, but simply follow their imagination, fits in with their being inefficient at recollecting. For recollection is not just a matter of having strings of images, but rather is an intellectual process, akin (453ª12–14) to deliberation.

453ª20 'The reason for recollecting not being under their control.' i.e. the reason why they can't prevent the search going on (453ª20–3), even after they have given up trying to recollect (453ª17–18).

453ª24 'Region': *topos*. The reference is to a part of the body, not to a part of the soul.

453^{a}25 'Takes a straight course.' According to *Phys.* 261^{a}27–263^{a}3 rectilinear motion, unlike circular, tends to stop.

453^{a}31–^{b}4 That the images fail to persist within after being imprinted, and that the movement set up during recollection is hard to stop, makes it sound as if these dwarf-like people have a lot of fluid in them. And indeed it is Aristotle's view that in such people one gets an unusually large amount of vapour surging upwards during the digestive processes (*Som.* 457^{a}24–5). In that case, the weight that rests on the perceptual organs will impede remembering in one way, while the fluidity will impede remembering in a different way, namely by preventing the persistence of images after they have been imprinted and by making it hard for the recollective motion to stop.

Alternatively, Aristotle may have in mind that the weight itself is responsible for impeding the persistence of images and for making it hard for the motion to stop. In that case, he will not be making use of the idea that dwarf-like people are fluid. And indeed in using the word 'also' in 453^{a}31 he may be distinguishing the class of dwarf-like people from the class of people (453^{a}23) who have excessive fluidity around the perceptual organs.

The changes that fail to persist within are the images imprinted at the time of the original learning or experience. As to why he should speak in terms of their being persistent rather than intermittent, see p. 16. 'From the start' means from the time of the original learning or experience. It is contrasted with 'during recollecting'.

453^{b}2 'The perceptive part.' I have supplied the noun 'part'. This time, Aristotle should be referring to a part of the body (cf. 453^{a}24), rather than to a part of the soul (cf. 450^{a}11; ^{a}14; ^{a}16; 451^{a}17; 453^{a}13). See notes on 449^{b}30 'That with which they perceive', and 450^{a}16–17.

453^{b}11 'What recollection is': chapter 2. 'In what manner' 451^{b}16–452^{b}7. 'Through what causes' 451^{b}10–16.

Textual Changes

The text followed in the main is that of W. D. Ross, in *Aristotle, Parva Naturalia*, a revised text with introduction and commentary, Oxford, 1955. But there are the following divergencies, mostly in favour of the mss. readings.

	W. D. ROSS	READING FOLLOWED
450ª10–11	transpose	* keep mss. order
450ª18	ἀνοήτων	* θνητῶν
450ª21	προσαισθάνεται ὅτι πρότερον	† πρότερον προσαισθάνεται
450ª30	delete τὸ πάθος	* keep
450ᵇ20	συμβαίνειν	* συμβαίνει
451ᵇ27–8	delete	* keep
452ª19	Α Β Γ Δ Ε ΖΗ ΘΙ	* Α Β Γ Δ Ε ΖΗ Θ
452ª20	Ι	* Θ
	Ε	† Ζ
452ª21	Δ	† Η
452ª22	Ζ --- Γ	* Ε --- Γ
452ª23	Α --- Β --- Η	* Δ --- Β --- Α
452ª26	Β	* Ζ
452ª27	διὰ πολλοῦ	* διὰ παλαιοῦ
452ᵇ15	delete καὶ τὰ ἐκτός	* keep

† Denotes emendation
* Denotes that the reading of some or all of the mss. has been preferred to emendations proposed or accepted by W. D. Ross.

Abbreviations

Cat.	*Categoriae*
Interp.	*De Interpretatione*
An. Pr.	*Analytica Priora*
An. Post.	*Analytica Posteriora*
Top.	*Topica*
Soph. El.	*De Sophisticis Elenchis*
Phys.	*Physica*
Cael.	*De Caelo*
G. & C.	*De Generatione et Corruptione*
Meteor.	*Meteorologica*
DA	*De Anima*
DS	*De Sensu et Sensibili*
DM	*De Memoria et Reminiscentia*
Som.	*De Somno et Vigilia*
Insom.	*De Insomniis*
Div.	*De Divinatione per Somnum*
Iuv.	*De Iuventute et Senectute, De Vita et Morte*
Resp.	*De Respiratione*
HA	*Historia Animalium*
PA	*De Partibus Animalium*
Motu	*De Motu Animalium*
GA	*De Generatione Animalium*
Probl.	*Problemata*
Metaph.	*Metaphysica*
NE	*Ethica Nicomachea*
EE	*Ethica Eudemia*
Pol.	*Politica*
Rhet.	*Rhetorica*
Fr.	(The reference here is to fragments, according to their line numbers in Bekker's edition of 1831.)

Select Bibliography

COMMENTARIES

Beare, J. I., Notes to his translation of the *De Memoria*, in *The Works of Aristotle*, transl. into English, edd. J. A. Smith and W. D. Ross, vol. III, Oxford, 1908.

Ross, G. R. T., *De Sensu et De Memoria*, text and transl., Cambridge, 1906.

Ross, W. D., *Aristotle, Parva Naturalia*, a revised text with introduction and commentary, Oxford, 1955.

Siwek, P., *Aristotelis Parva Naturalia, graece et latine*, Desclée, Rome, 1963.

St. Thomas Aquinas. *In Aristotelis Libros De Sensu et Sensato, De Memoria et Reminiscentia Commentarium*, Marietti, Turin and Rome, 1949.

MNEMONIC TECHNIQUES AND THE USE OF IMAGES

Allport, G. W., 'Eidetic Imagery', *British Journal of Psychology*, 1924.

Borges, Jorge Luis, 'Funes the Memorious', short story, translated in *Labyrinths, Selected Stories and Other Writings* by Jorge Luis Borges, ed. Donald A. Yates and James E. Irby, New York, 1962.

Galton, Francis, *Inquiries into Human Faculty*, London, 1883; 2nd edition 1907.

Haber, R. N., 'Eidetic Images', *Scientific American*, 1969.

Luria, A. R., 'Memory and the Structure of Mental Processes', in *Problems of Psychology* no. 1, Oxford, 1960.

Luria, A. R., *The Mind of a Mnemonist*, London/New York, 1969.

Post, L. A., 'Ancient Memory Systems', *Classical Weekly*, 1932.

Yates, Frances, *The Art of Memory*, London, 1966.

PLATO'S THEORY OF RECOLLECTION

Gulley, Norman, 'Plato's Theory of Recollection', *Classical Quarterly*, 1954.

Hoerber, Robert, 'Plato's *Meno*', *Phronesis*, 1960.

Rankin, H. D., 'Immediate Cognition of the Forms in the Phaedo?', *Dialectica*, 1958.

Vlastos, Gregory, '*Anamnesis* in the *Meno*', *Dialogue*, 1965.

ACCOUNTS OF MEMORY TO BE COMPARED WITH ARISTOTLE'S

James, William, *The Principles of Psychology*, vol. 1, New York and London, 1890.

Malcolm, Norman, 'Memory and Representation', *Nous*, 1970.

Martin, C. B., and Deutscher, Max, 'Remembering,' *The Philosophical Review*, 1966.

Mill, James, *Analysis of the Phenomena of the Human Mind*, 1st edition 1829; new edition London, 1869, vol. 1.

Plotinus, Enneads IV. 6.

Reid, Thomas, *Essays on the Intellectual Powers of Man*, ed. Woozley, London, 1941, Essay III.

Russell, Bertrand, *The Analysis of Mind*, London, 1921.

THE RELATION OF BODY AND SOUL IN ARISTOTLE

Kahn, Charles, 'Sensation and Consciousness in Aristotle's Psychology', *Archiv für Geschichte der Philosophie*, 1966.

Sorabji, Richard, 'Body and Soul in Aristotle', forthcoming.

Index